CASTLETON
VERMONT

CASTLETON
VERMONT

ITS INDUSTRIES, ENTERPRISES & EATERIES

DONALD H. THOMPSON

THE History PRESS

Published by The History Press
Charleston, SC 29403
www.historypress.net

Front cover images: Painting of Castleton Village by James Hope. *Courtesy of the Castleton Historical Society.* MacRae Orchard apple picking and packing crew. *Courtesy of Jane Griffin.*
Back cover images: *Arthur B. Cook* steamer. *Courtesy of the author.* Brown's Roadside Market. *Courtesy of Elizabeth Patch Wilkinson.* Staso Milling site. *Courtesy of Mary Beth Hadeka.*

First published 2010

Manufactured in the United States

ISBN 978.1.60949.096.6

Library of Congress Cataloging-in-Publication Data

Thompson, Donald H.
Castleton, Vermont : its industries, enterprises and eateries / Donald H. Thompson.
p. cm.
Includes bibliographical references and index.
ISBN 978-1-60949-096-6
1. Castleton (Vt.)--History. 2. Business enterprises--Vermont--Castleton. 3. Castleton (Vt.)--Economic conditions. I. Title.
F59.C3T46 2010
338.09743'7--dc22
2010035214

CONTENTS

ACKNOWLEDGEMENTS

I would like to thank the following people who helped me with interviews, photographs, technical help and information. The dates in parentheses indicate when the interview took place. My sincere apologies to anyone I might have omitted from this list:

Bob Barnes (June 2010), Lloyd Bronson Jr. (July 2009), Eileen Brough, John Brough Jr. (June 2010), Charles Brown (July 2010), Joan Brown (June 2010), Steve Brown, Danielle Woodard Budlong, Claire Burditt, David Camara, Castleton Community Center staff, Castleton State College Library staff, Eileen Colburn (May 2010), Bonnie Crossman, Judy Crowley, Beverly Davidson, Joseph Doran, Ennis Duling, John Durfee, Agnes Earls, Bill Earls, Roger Ellis (June 2010), Bonnie Ennis (June 2010), Pat and Dave Finlayson (June 2010), Ken Flowers, Janet Macomber Foley (June 2010), Fran Grey (May 2010), Jane Griffin (May 2010), Mary Beth Hadeka, Caren Helm (May 2010), Bill Jenkins, Tom Kearns, Tim and Lorraine Keller (June 2010), Bernice Kelly, Joe and Liz Kent, Mary Jo Knapp (July 2009), Kevin and Lori Knauer (June 2010), George and Elizabeth Lamphere, Bob and Sadie Laramie (June 2010), James Leamy (December 2009), Pam Maccabee, George Merkel (July 2010), Kathleen Mulligan (December 2009), John O'Day (November 2009), Chip Ogg (August 2009), Robert Page, Mel Patch (June 2010), Phototec, Valerie Poremski (May 2010), Gordon and Joanne Ringquist (August 2009), Dave Rogers, Roz Rogers (June 2010), Michael

Rosen, Edward Ryan (July 2008), Steve Schild of Rutland Regional Planning Commission, Donald Sevigny (May 2010), Joe Sessock (June 2010), Dallas and Anne Skinner, Dave Socinksi, Linda Splatt, Buddy and Pat Taggart (May 2010), Carol A. Thomson, Paul Thompson, Jerome Towers, Frederick Waite, Elizabeth Patch Wilkinson (June 2010), Rick Wilson, Ron Wilson, Paul Wiskoski and Betty Zahnleiter (June 2010).

INTRODUCTION

In the process of writing this book, I interviewed nearly thirty people who graciously and generously shared their knowledge and memories of the businesses, eateries and country stores that have been a part of Castleton, Vermont's long history. Everyone leads busy lives, and at times, it was hard to catch up with people. However, their willingness to make time to talk to me and to share information and photos has been gratifying and much appreciated. It is my hope that readers unfamiliar with the history of places such as Coon's Store and Uncle Charlie's Restaurant will find the story of its transformations over the years interesting. Many of the establishments described in the book are a tribute to their owners' perseverance and hard work. I personally find the human-interest stories, such as that of apple picker Sadie Laramie, both interesting and inspirational. The more I found out, the more I wanted to learn about Castleton's past. Its history belies the picturesque, college-town image that someone casually passing through might infer today.

The book traces the establishment of the town by original settlers Colonel Amos Bird and Noah Lee (who in 1767 trekked through untamed wilderness) to the building of mills and small industries along the Castleton River, the development of the slate industry, the coming of the railroad and finally, the commercial establishments that thrive today in Castleton. Castleton was a busy, bustling community in bygone eras. The variety of commercial enterprises over the past 243 years is astonishing. Many current residents may not know the town once had a plow factory, an iron stove works and, like its neighbor Fair Haven, produced beautiful marbleized slate, now a lost art. Many of the small factories, such as the slate pencil mill, became victims to progress. The railroad proved to be both a positive and negative influence; on one hand, it enabled local products to be shipped to more distant markets, but it also brought in lower-priced competing products.

In researching and writing the book, I am especially grateful for help from Roz Rogers, Claire Burditt, Elizabeth Patch Wilkinson, Mel Patch and especially my wife, Carol, who has once again put many hours into typing, proofreading and otherwise attending to technical aspects, besides making helpful suggestions for wording and helping the book to flow smoothly.

Chapter 1

PIONEERS AND EARLY INDUSTRIES

Mills to Apples

The Mills of Castleton

Castleton came into existence in 1761, when Benning Wentworth, governor of the New Hampshire Grants, issued sixty charters in the name of Great Britain's King George III. One of these thirty-six-square-mile tracts was designated as the Township of Castleton. Of the available land, five hundred acres were reserved for Governor Wentworth, and sixty-four individuals received seventy shares. The charter provided for things such as an annual meeting, the right to hold a market, two fairs once fifty families had settled and rights for a church and school.

In the spring of 1767, Colonel Amos Bird, Noah Lee and a "colored servant" set out from Salisbury, Connecticut, to survey the Township of Castleton. Their journey north was far from direct, however. They traveled from Bennington, Vermont, to Manchester, where they followed a trail of blazed trees to Clarendon. Upon reaching Rutland, they took the old military road (Crown Point Road) west to Crown Point, New York. They were "wholly ignorant of the fact that they passed along the northern border of Castleton." They stopped at Ticonderoga, where they replenished their provisions and continued south to Skenesboro, which is now Whitehall, New York. Finally, they arrived in Castleton in June 1767, covering a lot of territory that used to be wilderness. They spent the summer surveying

Castleton. Tradition holds that Bird got lost and found himself atop a mountain in the eastern part of Castleton. He spent the night there, and the mountain has been called Bird Mountain ever since.

Before returning to Salisbury, Connecticut, for the winter, Bird and Lee built a log cabin on a bluff just south of present-day Castleton Corners, near the original east–west road that follows the Castleton River. The following spring, the three men returned to Castleton with the intention of starting a permanent settlement. They continued surveying over that summer and cleared forest land, but they did not plant any crops. Amos Bird returned to Connecticut before winter set in, but Noah Lee and the servant stayed all winter, living in the log cabin and enduring much hardship. The winter of 1768–1769 was severe, with extreme cold and heavy snow. The servant's feet nearly froze, and they ran short of provisions. The river remained frozen, so they had little luck fishing, and their weapons were in poor condition, which made hunting difficult as well. Tradition says the two men actually chased down game on their snowshoes. Somehow, they survived.

There has been speculation on the origin of the new settlement's name. There was no town by that name within the American colonies prior to 1761, when Benning Wentworth issued the sixty charters. It did not get its name from any of the early settlers or grantees, since none were named Castle. The most probable explanation is that it was named after a place in the British Isles, where several towns named Castleton existed. The prime candidate for the town's name is the Castleton found in Derbyshire, England, the place from where Noah Lee's ancestors originated prior to immigrating to Massachusetts Bay Colony in 1634. The Lee family was prominent in Salisbury, Connecticut, and Noah Lee was not only one of the first Castleton, Vermont settlers, he went on to become one of the town's most-distinguished citizens.

When Amos Bird, Noah Lee and the servant arrived, Castleton was a wilderness with no roads, dwellings or other structures. The only other humans in the area were the Abenaki Indians, who fished and hunted along the shores of Lake Bomoseen. Amos Bird owned forty of the original seventy Castleton shares. In 1771, he and nine men erected a sawmill at the outlet of Lake Bomoseen. The location was known as Castleton Mills, which is now Hydeville. In 1772, when Bird died prematurely of pneumonia at age thirty-one, the mill provided the pine boards for his coffin. Settlers had begun arriving around that time. Three families came in 1770, and by 1777, the village had grown to seventeen houses, although a Hessian officer during the American Revolution described them as "miserable." He also mentioned plentiful trout and rattlesnakes and found rattlesnake soup "palatable."

In the early years prior to 1830, Castleton settlers had to be hardworking and self-sufficient. They had large families who worked together to clear the wilderness and plant crops. Many originally came from Connecticut, and they used oxen brought from there for plowing. The earliest settlers had little to sell or barter, so they relied on what they could do with their own hands and ingenuity. As more settlers came, they began to specialize in their skills: women spun yarn and made cloth at home; blacksmiths shod horses and forged nails and iron implements; and a cobbler provided shoes. Shops and businesses began to grow up in Castleton to fulfill the needs of the growing community.

The first east–west road through the village of Castleton followed the Castleton River. In 1772, Noah Lee was one member of a committee to change the road so that it went through the pine-covered plain west of Castleton Corners, where Route 4A is today. He was also part of the committee to lay out a north–south highway, which is now the East Hubbardton Road. Lee, unlike his friend Amos Bird, lived to the ripe old age of ninety-four. In his long life, he witnessed the growth of Castleton from a few hardy settlers to almost two thousand souls by 1840, when he died. He not only had a long life but a productive and distinguished one. He fought in the French and Indian War, including at Crown Point in 1761. At the start of the Revolutionary War, he returned to Connecticut, enlisted in the Continental army and achieved the rank of captain. Lee participated in several major battles, including Brandywine and Trenton, and witnessed the surrender at Yorktown. He was awarded three hundred acres of land in Ohio for his service. He returned to Vermont after the war and became a colonel in the militia. He also served as a delegate to the Constitutional Convention in 1791. He and his wife, Dorcas, had eight children and lived on what is now Route 4A near the Castleton River.

In the 1790s, two dams were constructed at the outlet to Lake Bomoseen. The upper dam provided water power to run a forge and ironworks. The lower dam ran a gristmill and the sawmill, built by Amos Bird, which continued in operation after his death, provided lumber for the waves of new settlers building homes and barns. By 1829, there were three sawmills, the gristmill, a carding machine and two clothiers' works at Hydeville. The fertile soil of western and southern Castleton was conducive to growing grain, which was sent to be ground at the gristmill at the outlet of Lake Bomoseen. In 1803, Erastus Higley and Ebenezer Langdon built mills on the Castleton River to grind grain, make linseed oil and card woolen fibers for making cloth. In the same mill, Solomon Guernsey had a lathe to turn out things such as cider mill screws, bedsteads and other furniture items.

In the early 1800s, sheep raising came into its own in Vermont, with more than a million Merino sheep grazing on the hillsides throughout the state. Castleton had its share of the wool industry, with fleece being brought to be machine carded at the water-powered mills on the river. Local mill owners prospered, particularly during the War of 1812, due to a tariff that discouraged importation of competing foreign cloth. However, after the War of 1812, sheep production declined, and so did Castleton's woolen industry.

Another industry that flourished for several decades in the Castleton area was iron working, using local bog iron. Matthew Lyon's ironworks was already producing nails and other iron items as early as 1785 in the Fair Haven area. In 1835, Selah Hart Langdon began to manufacture iron stoves on Mill Street by the Castleton River, which provided water power. The S.H. Langdon furnace is likely the one shown just off Mill Street on the 1869 map. An example of the type of stove manufactured by S.L. Langdon is pictured in this section.

By 1851, the Foundry and Agricultural Implement Manufacturing Company, operated by Francis Barrows, was producing plows for area farmers at its shop in Castleton Corners. Later, Sargents' Plow Manufacturing continued the manufacture of plows on the same site, which is now the location of the Citgo gas station on the northwest corner of the intersection of Routes 30 and 4A.

In the 1870s, another company, the Agricultural Implement Manufacturing Company of Hydeville, also produced farm equipment. Eventually all of these small, local iron foundries lost their market, due to competition from larger outside companies that produced cheaper products, and went out of business.

In 1774, Nehemiah Hoyt bought land at the corner of present-day Main Street and Cemetery Road in Castleton. Twenty years later, Enos Merrill dammed the small stream that emptied into the Castleton River and created a millpond to run a tannery and cobbler shop. A brick building was erected around 1800 to house these two endeavors, and it stands today as Vermont's oldest brick structure. It now serves as a museum and is run by

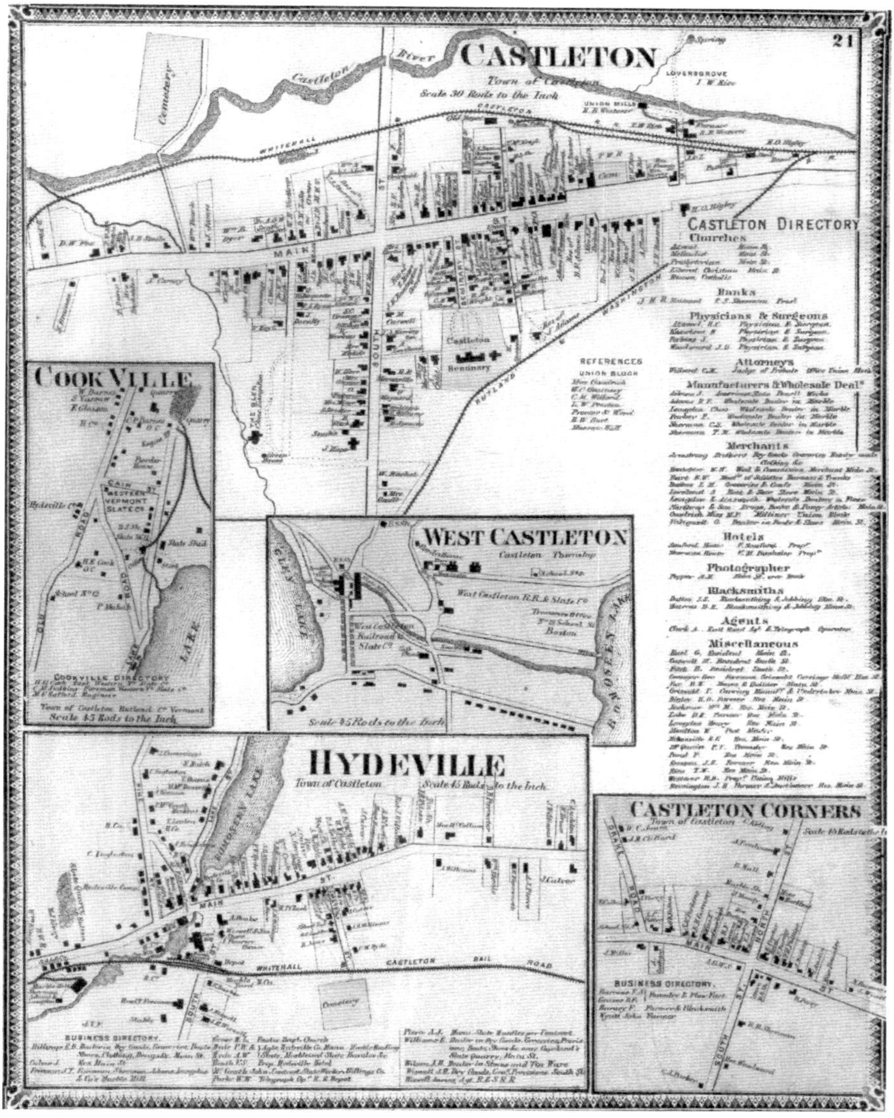

Maps of Rutland County, Vermont, in 1869. *Courtesy of* Beers Atlas.

the Castleton Historical Society; it is open to visitors during special events. Bark and sumac were put into the millpond as part of the tanning process, and the tanned hides were taken into the cobbler shop, where Enos Merrill made shoes, using metal lasts to shape and size them. A photo in this section

Left: Langdon Iron Stove. *Courtesy of Castleton Historical Society.*

Below: The cobbler shop and tannery, circa 1910. *Courtesy of Castleton Historical Society.*

shows the cobbler shop around 1910, when it was the home of John James and family.

In the 1830s, Castleton became a central point in the stagecoach business that had begun to develop in southwestern Vermont. First E.B. Dewey and later Arunah Hyde in 1835 became stage coach proprietors for the mail service from Albany to Burlington and other destinations. When the railroad was built from Whitehall, New York, to Rutland, Vermont, in 1850, Castleton's status as a transportation center dropped to become just a way station along the rail line.

By the 1840s, there were an increasing number of marble and slate mills located near water power in the area. However, the mill owners found they had no convenient means of water transportation by which to ship their finished products. Zadock Thompson, in his 1824 *Gazetteer of the State of Vermont,* suggested the Castleton River be used to connect Otter Creek and Lake Champlain by building an eighteen-mile canal. A circa-1860s drawing in this section shows a canal boat on a canal running through Castleton and several landmarks, including the Congregational Church, depot and seminary in the background, but the proposed canal was never built.

Transportation difficulties experienced early on by the mills were resolved by the construction of two railroads that intersected at the Castleton depot that still exists today. In 1847, the Rutland and Washington Railroad Company started a line ostensibly to connect Rutland, Vermont, with Whitehall, New York; however, the company directors decided to connect with Troy, New

Drawing of the canal through Castleton. *Courtesy of Ken Flowers.*

The Delaware and Hudson depot in Castleton. *Courtesy of Linda Splatt.*

York, instead and turned the tracks south at Castleton. Service began in October 1850. Railroad interests in Whitehall were displeased with this change; so in 1848, another railroad company was formed—the Rutland and Whitehall—that built track from Rutland through Castleton and Fair Haven to the New York State line, running west from a connection in Castleton. Both of these rail lines eventually became part of the Delaware and Hudson Railroad.

The building of the railroad lines encouraged growth of the local slate and marble industries, as now there was an economically feasible way to get their heavy products to market. The combination of available water power and rail transportation brought a burst of economic activity, especially to towns with depots such as Castleton and Hydeville. By the 1880s, there were more than fifteen quarries operating in Hydeville, Blissville, Cooksville, West Castleton, Poultney and Fair Haven. In Hydeville alone, there were two marble companies and four slate companies, as well as a flour mill, lumber mill, cobbler shop, wagon maker, hardware store and two grocery stores. When large hotels were built around Lake Bomoseen in the latter half of the nineteenth century, the local communities continued to benefit, as numbers of visitors came to the area for recreation. Summer visitors would arrive by train at Hydeville or Castleton and be delivered by wagon or steamboat to their final destinations at the resorts farther up the lake.

The Vermont Pie Belt

From almost its earliest settlement until today, apples have been an important business in Vermont. A 1794 deed and a road survey from 1802 both mention the existence of an apple orchard in Hydeville, where the Hydeville plaza and post office are today. Alexander Dunnehue, a tinsmith living in the area, requested to be buried beneath his apple tree so he could catch the boys trying to steal his apples. He may have gotten his wish, as there was a cemetery noted near the orchard on the 1802 survey. From the 1700s through the late 1800s, the focus had been on clearing land for pasture and farming, but as open land began to decline around 1900, newspaper articles, in which farmers were encouraged to grow apples as a profitable crop, started appearing. The *Poultney Journal* declared in its August 30, 1909 edition that "lying in the New England pie belt in a region where the apple reaches its greatest perfection, Vermont ought to be the center of the American apple industry. There are thousands of acres of rocky hills in the state that are now practically useless that will raise the finest apples in the world." For many years, most farmers had maintained small orchards for their own use, resulting in twenty-three varieties that originated in Vermont. By the turn of the twentieth century, some of the apples were becoming rare: Blakely and Rum from Pawlet, Highlander from Sudbury and the Pownal Spitzenburg are varieties no longer found. Few people today are familiar with these and other heirloom apples, such as Sheep's Nose, named for its bulge, and the softball-sized Wolf River, so large that it was said a pie could be made with just one.

In September, 1939, the *Rutland Herald* reported:

> *50,000 apple trees in a dozen Rutland and Addison County towns were estimated here today to be laden with 200,000 bushels of fruit ready to harvest and valued at approximately $350,000. McIntoshes predominate, but other varieties grown in the area are Wealthy, Delicious, Greenings, Northern Spy apples...The bulk of the crop is grown in Fair Haven, Castleton, Orwell, Shoreham, and Poultney.*

Some of the local orchards at the time were Ellis Orchard, Griffin Orchard, Paolino's Heaven Hill Orchard and the MacRae Orchard, one of the largest in the Castleton area.

Apple packing house crew at MacCrae Orchard. *Courtesy of Mel Patch.*

The MacRae Orchard was located adjacent to Lake Bomoseen, east of what is now Indian Point Road. During the 1920s and '30s, the MacRae Orchard had thirteen thousand trees, most of which were the McIntosh variety, which commanded a high price in the New York and Boston markets. It employed a large crew of seasonal workers to harvest and pack the fruit. The two large packing buildings are still standing along Drake Road, just north of the Route 4 highway bridge. In more recent times, the former packinghouses have been used for a variety of purposes, from dance halls to antique auctions. During the 1940s, the *Rutland Herald* often ran announcements of barn dances at the MacRae Orchard, often to benefit the American Legion post.

Not all of the apple crop from MacRae's was shipped to large urban centers like New York City. The MacRae orchard sold apples at a stand located on the corner of Drake Road and present-day Route 4A.

In 1946, then owner John Wells sold the orchard to the Jamac Company. At the time, there were only about six thousand trees left producing apples, and the new owners never got it up and running again. In the 1970s, the new Route 4 highway cut through the orchard. Early pictures show it was

Panoramic view of MacCrae Orchard. *Courtesy of Mel Patch.*

an extensive property that stretched from the southeastern end of the lake to well beyond present-day Drake Road. The MacRae trees are nearly all gone today. A few stragglers remain here and there along Drake and Indian Point Roads. While most of these once-flourishing local orchards that dotted the countryside are no longer in existence, apples are still grown in the region, particularly in the Champlain Valley. Apple picking remains a popular fall pastime for local families and visitors alike.

Another orchard located in Castleton was owned by the Griffin family for three generations. This orchard, located in the southern part of the town, was started in 1931 by Charles E. Griffin. He moved his family into a house built in 1854. He planted McIntosh, Red Delicious and Northern Spy apples on sixty acres of land. These varieties were planted in alternating rows to increase pollination by honeybees. Charles Griffin's son Wray doubled the size of the orchard, adding sixty more acres, and ran it until his death in 1961. The following year, the Griffins purchased thirty more acres from the Ward family and referred to this new section as the Pond Hill Block. A nine-foot fence was erected around the orchard to keep out the deer.

At first, the Griffin Orchard sold all of its production to a broker in New York City. In 1960, the family built a packinghouse, which was followed by a cold storage building in 1965. The new facility allowed apples to be stored from September through the end of January. During this time, they exported apples to England, which required the apples to be sealed and tagged by inspectors for shipment. For a while, their business was insured against hail damage by Lloyd's of London, but it eventually became too costly. After that, they sold hail-damaged apples to the Beechnut Company in Canandaigua, New York, to be made into applesauce and juice.

During the 1970s, there was a scarcity of local laborers, so the Griffins imported Jamaicans to pick the apples. These workers arrived in early September and stayed through the end of October. The Griffins provided local housing and kept the Jamaican workers happy with meals of their preference, including goat meat, which was a favorite dish.

Wray Griffin's son, Bruce, and his wife, Jane, celebrated the fiftieth anniversary of the orchard's existence with a grand party at the Trak-In on July 12, 1981. Today, many of the trees remain, but the orchard is no longer in business.

Jamaican apple picker at Griffin Orchard. *Courtesy of Jane Griffin.*

Sadie and Bob Laramie, both in their eighties today, were apple pickers at both the Allen Orchard in Fair Haven and the Ellis Orchard in Castleton in the late 1940s to 1950. Sadie describes a typical day as an apple picker:

> *We would work from 7:00 in the morning until 5:00 or 6:00 at night, until the last tree was picked clean. If there was frost the night before, we'd wait until around 9:00 a.m. to start. The trees were taller at Ellis, so there I'd be up on a twenty-foot ladder. I'd pick my way out to the road, and see no one till noon. Then we got half an hour for lunch. We picked every day, for about seven weeks. The pay back then was ten cents a bushel. I averaged 110 bushels a day, but my record number of bushels picked in one day was 136. We picked different varieties as they were ready—Cortland, McIntosh, Delicious, Northern Spy and a few "winter banana," a variety that was hard and kept well. At the end of the season I'd made about five hundred dollars, which was used to pay for our winter fuel.*

Sadie went on to mention they had eleven children, so to help support them she also worked evenings at the Fair Haven Outlet after finishing her ten-hour day picking apples. She reported proudly that the children all turned out well, and she and Bob recently celebrated their sixtieth wedding anniversary.

Chapter 2

THE GROWTH OF CASTLETON'S SCHOOLS AND BUSINESSES

During the late eighteenth and nineteenth centuries, a variety of businesses and educational institutions grew up in the village of Castleton. As early as 1786, "Samuel Moulton leased one acre of land to the inhabitants of Castleton for a term of 500 years to erect, build and set up a schoolhouse…for teaching and instructing…and no other purpose." The corporation of Rutland County Grammar School erected a new schoolhouse, but it burned down in 1805. It was replaced by another school called the Academy. In 1855, another building was erected, known as the Grammar School and Town Hall, with the town hall on the upper story and the school on the bottom floor. This building existed until 1952, when it was demolished, and the present-day Village School was built on the site. The clock on top of the Town Hall and School was preserved and found a new home atop the Castleton Village Library, where it remains today.

Besides these schools, by 1818, Castleton could boast an institution of higher learning with the opening of the Castleton Medical Academy, later called Castleton Medical College. Within a year, there were twenty-four students and four instructors. In 1822, a new building was erected on the west corner of Main Street and North Road, the site of St. John's Roman Catholic Church today. The old building was moved and attached to the new one to provide dormitory rooms. The new two-story building had a lecture room, laboratory, study room and library on the first floor. On the second

Students in front of Grammar School and Town Hall. *Courtesy of Betty Zahnleiter.*

floor, there were an "anatomical theater," a lecture room and a dissecting room. A cupola with a bell and clock were added to adorn the roof.

At first degrees were actually conferred by Middlebury College, as the Vermont legislature had forgotten a provision in the school's charter that allowed it to grant degrees. That was rectified two years later. By 1862, about 1,400 men had received medical training there to become doctors; at that time women were not allowed to enroll. In spite of so many graduates in a relatively short span, the medical college was closed in the spring of 1862 after several years of various problems, including conflict among the trustees, dropping enrollment and financial problems. With the difficulties of the Civil War, the college was never reopened, and in 1865, Carlos Sherman gave the building to the principal of the Castleton Seminary. It was then moved up the hill and placed next to the Seminary Building. At one time, it had wings on either side, but they are no longer in existence. In 1968, the old medical college building was moved down the hill to where it is located today.

An interesting fact about medical schools in the nineteenth century is that cadavers, used for learning anatomy and surgical skills, were scarce.

The medical college building, next to the Castleton Normal School. *Courtesy of the author.*

There were several medical schools within Vermont from 1820 to 1840, and it has been estimated that about 1,600 students dissected around 400 cadavers. Without a reliable source of cadavers, students resorted to grave robbing at times. The State of Vermont was slow to enact laws forbidding this practice until incidents involving students from the medical schools in Woodstock and Castleton created a public outcry. One such incident has gone down in history as "The Hubbardton Raid." In November 1830, two medical students from Castleton Medical Collage disinterred a woman named Penfield Churchill from a cemetery in Hubbardton. At about 9:00 a.m. on Monday, November 29, 1830, about 300 men, in three groups, one led by the sheriff of the county, marched the five miles from Hubbardton to Castleton and surrounded the medical college.

The story becomes even more macabre; while the college dean stalled the crowd, the medical students proceeded to remove the head from the body, presumably to prevent identification, and concealed the body below the floorboards. Meanwhile, one of the students escaped out the back door, with the head under his coat. The students almost got away with their deed, as there was no sign of the body when the irate crowd was allowed entrance. However, by sheer bad luck for the students, one of the men stumbled on the loose floor board, which led to the discovery of the body. The college ultimately expelled the two grave robbers to appease public outrage. The authorities agreed to drop charges if the head was returned. Few students today are aware that the dignified medical college building, now used for lectures and meetings, once witnessed dissections of bodies stolen from local cemeteries. Only a few items in the display cases, such as surgical tools, hint at the building's past.

The Castleton Seminary began shortly after the medical college in the 1830s. The name might lead one to suppose it was a theological institution, but, unlike today, the term seminary also referred to any institution of higher learning. Seminaries for young ladies were common, for example. The Castleton Seminary was located on the top of the hill at the end of Seminary Street. In 1876, it was decided to rename the school Castleton Normal School, which served for the training of schoolteachers. The name came from the French term for teacher-training schools, *ecole normal.*

Caroline Woodruff, principal of Castleton Normal School in the 1920s, became one of Vermont's most distinguished educators. She was instrumental in improving the curriculum and staff. It is fitting that, when the building burned in 1924, the new building was named in her honor. Woodruff Hall is still a landmark on campus today. In the 1930s, Woodruff was named the first female president of the National Education Association, the only Vermonter ever to hold that position.

Sports programs began at the college in the 1950s, with men's baseball and basketball for both men and women. The following decade saw major growth and expansion at Castleton's institution of higher learning, now called Castleton State College. Degrees were offered in several disciplines besides teaching. In 1965, Huden Dining Hall, Haskell Hall and Adams Hall were added. The Fine Arts Center opened in 1969, providing a place for theater arts and music programs. It also benefits the community through hosting a variety of concerts and plays that are open to the public. Fire destroyed Leavenworth Hall in 1971, but it was rebuilt on the same site. Since then, the Calvin Coolidge Library has been expanded, and the Stafford Science Center and Babcock Hall have been added. The latest addition to the campus is the new Spartan Stadium, which is home to Castleton State College's new football team; it had its first season in 2009. The stadium also is used by the field hockey, lacrosse and soccer teams. In 2009, the Campus Center was also completely renovated, and the gymnasium was enlarged. Leavenworth

The Castleton State College campus in 1971. *Courtesy of Castleton State College Archives.*

Newly completed Spartan Stadium in the fall of 2009. *Courtesy of Castleton State College Archives.*

Hall recently acquired a new television studio. The student population is currently 1,800 students, and roughly half of whom live on campus, either in the seven residence halls or three on-campus houses. About 63 percent of the students are Vermont residents. The college offers more than thirty programs, including liberal arts, sciences, nursing and teaching.

The Business District

Castleton Village had a variety of retail stores to serve its growing population of 2,605, according to the 1880 census. Shortly after the turn of the twentieth century, the village was plagued by four separate and very destructive fires that demolished stores, businesses and a large hotel. In July 1904, the *Fair Haven Era* reported that the Union block, the largest business block in the village, was totally destroyed by fire. The two-story brick building had housed the E.H. Armstrong drugstore, the Beach and Lee dry-goods store, John Fennell's meat market and grocery store, the Charles Ryan bakery and an Italian shoe shop. Upstairs were the rooms of the Masonic Hall (Lee Lodge) and the Bomoseen Grange Hall. The building was partially insured, and the individual businesses carried some insurance. The Union block building was replaced by the Trudell block on the south side of Main Street. It contained a barbershop, E.N. Northrop's drugstore and A.L. Ransom's hardware store. The Masonic Hall and Bomoseen Grange had relocated upstairs. Unfortunately, on Easter Sunday 1917, this building too burned down.

A photo in this section, taken sometime before 1912, shows the Castleton Post Office, a small brick building, and then the taller brick Trudell Block. The building with large columns on the right is the Sanford House. The left-hand side of the Trudell Block held a barbershop on the ground floor, evidenced by the typical striped barber's pole. Northrop's drugstore occupied the center section, with its trademark mortar and pestle sign. A.L. Ransom's hardware store was on the west side of the building, but at the time of the photo, it appeared to be vacant.

The 1890s view of Main Street shows the Liddell block and two houses on the left side. This spot is where the Castleton Free Library is located today. The church spire of the Liberal Christian Church and the Bomoseen House, a hotel, can be seen beyond the houses. Miss Wardlow's Millinery Shop and

The Trudell Block on south side of Main Street, looking west. *Courtesy of Linda Splatt.*

The north side of Main Street in Castleton, looking east, circa early 1890s. *Courtesy of Castleton Historical Society.*

John Moriarty's Castleton Meat and Provision Market were on the south side of Main Street at the corner of Seminary Street until the 1917 fire.

On November 7, 1912, the *Fair Haven Era* reported that the Bomoseen House and A.L. Ransom Store had burned down: "The fire started shortly after 7 o'clock in the hotel kitchen and the entire structure was soon ablaze." The nearest firefighting equipment that was available was in Rutland, and it could not respond fast enough to save the buildings. The Bomoseen House, built in 1868, could accommodate one hundred guests and was owned at various times by Horace B. Ellis and William C. Mound, who were associated with Lake Bomoseen hotels as well. The A.L. Ransom Country Store, which was located on the corner of Main Street and Mechanic Street, had been in business for thirty years. Its west wall survived and has been incorporated into the addition to the Birdseye Diner, which is found at the intersection of Main Street and Mechanic Street. The loss of both businesses was estimated to be about $50,000, but there were no reports of casualties due to the fire. A rare close-up photo of the Bomoseen House was featured in a souvenir booklet of Castleton, Vermont, postmarked August 1905. It had a grandeur not seen in modern-day hotels. The structure behind the hotel usually cannot be seen in most old photos looking down Main Street.

The Bomoseen House, with C.B. Webster as its proprietor, in a postcard dated 1906.
Courtesy of the author.

Prior to 1900, if you were to travel west along Main Street in Castleton, you would pass the Rumsey–St. John Feed Store, the Sanford House, the F.L. Reed Hardware Store and the Marcus Langdon House. On July 4, 1913, a fire destroyed this section of South Main Street. Only the feed store survived. Today, this building exists as the Merwin Gallery. The Pizza Place and Blue Cat Bistro, as well as the Castleton Village Store, occupy the site of the former Sanford House. The site of F.L. Reed's Hardware Store is where the Masonic Hall exists today.

The Long Block, which is located on the northwest corner of Main and Mechanic Streets, survived the 1912 fire; various stores and businesses, including a small restaurant, have occupied the first floor. Today, the building is owned by John and Pam Rehlen, and it previously housed a photo processing center. Today it is occupied by two businesses, Simply Antiques and Special Effects Unisex Hair Salon. In the far left background of a photo showing Ransom's store is the steeple of the Methodist Episcopal Church, before it was moved across Main Street.

One of the few early buildings in the village not consumed by fire is the Castleton Town Office building, which was built in 1834. That year, John Meacham sold Julian Buel fifteen feet of frontage with the provision that

The Long Block and A.L. Ransom's store on Main Street in Castleton. *Courtesy of Linda Splatt.*

The Long Block today on North Main Street, looking east. *Courtesy of the author.*

Mr. Meacham would erect a building along the boundary line and permit Mr. Buel to build onto its west wall. The next year, Ezekiel Buell deeded Julian use of the east wall of his hat shop for the west wall of Julian's law office. Therefore, the entire building was constructed by three different men at three different times. Later occupants were the Bank of Castleton, Judge Henry L. Clark's probate office, the Castleton Library and the Castleton Historical Society Museum. Today it is the home of Castleton's municipal offices and the police department.

Castleton has had a number of churches during its existence. There were as many as six different congregations. The Methodist Episcopal Church, which was built in 1824, the First Liberal Christian-Universalist, 1868, and the Congregational Church, 1833, were all on North Main Street. The Catholic Church took over the Universalist Church in 1879, and after it burned, the parish built St. John the Baptist Roman Catholic Church in 1893. Not quite a hundred years later, in 1970, the present-day St. John's Roman Catholic Church was built on the north side of Main Street. On the south side of Main Street were two other churches: the Second Advent Church, which was built in 1861, and St. Mark's Episcopal Church, 1899.

The Probate Office, which is now Castleton Town Offices. *Courtesy of Castleton Historical Society.*

While the casual observer may note that today there are only three churches in operation on Main Street—the Castleton Federated Church, St. John's Roman Catholic Church and St. Mark's Episcopal Church—several former church buildings have not faded from sight. Instead, they have undergone a transformation. The 1893 Roman Catholic Church has been a private residence and art studio. The 1861 Second Advent Church was used for a community center, art studio and residence. The 1824 Methodist Episcopal Church, originally located on the north side of Main Street, was moved to the other side of the street. The back of the church became the front of the building. Over the years this same building has been occupied by various businesses, including a Grand Union supermarket. At one time it was a social center operated by the local Roman Catholic Church; it is now home to Citizens Bank. It is interesting to note how many of Castleton's early structures were "recycled" over the years.

The tallest building in Castleton—until it was demolished in 2000—was Harold Brown's feed mill, which was found off Mill Street. It was common for millworkers to come into stores covered with flour dust. A Brown family story relates how a fortuneteller predicted Harold Brown's future wife, Helen, would marry a man all in white, possibly covered with snow. It wasn't snow,

The Methodist Episcopal Church, which is now Citizens Bank. *Courtesy of Castleton Historical Society.*

but flour, as it turned out. She met him at the mill, and they were married not long afterward.

A late 1940s photograph shows a view of Castleton, looking east. Some of the buildings pictured will be familiar to present-day visitors. From left are an Esso gas station and shops then owned by Harry Kinney, which are now the site of the Pizza Place and Blue Cat Bistro. The store next to the gas station is recognizable as today's Castleton Village Store, previously Ballard's and before that Wright's. The two-story brick building in the picture was once the post office and Eddy's Market. Today, it houses the Castleton Laundromat and Riley's Insurance. The large three-story building is the Castleton Garage, with Tydol gasoline pumps in front. Betty Zahnleiter's grandfather built the Castleton Garage during the late 1920s. She and her family lived upstairs during the 1930s. She recalls that next door to the garage, to the right, was a small restaurant that later was moved to Hart Towers Road on Lake Bomoseen for use as a cottage. The Castleton Garage was the scene of the village's last major fire, which took place in the 1950s. Later, another small garage was built there that now stands vacant. More recently, its empty parking lot has served as the location for Castleton's weekly farmers' market.

South Main Street, circa the late 1940s. *Courtesy of the author.*

Four girls in front of restaurant on Main Street in Castleton. *Courtesy of Betty Zahnleiter.*

One of the more intriguing twentieth century enterprises attempted in Castleton was a ski center located on Birdseye Mountain. Many residents and visitors today are probably unaware it existed. In 1961, Bill Jenkins, director of physical education at Green Mountain College in Poultney, thought a beginner- and intermediate-level ski area would benefit college students and the surrounding communities. He and a group of directors chose the north slope of Bird (or Birdseye, as it is called locally) Mountain, near where the towns of Ira and Castleton meet, as a good, easily accessible site. The lodge, containing a restaurant, ski shop and a small beginner slope with a rope tow, opened in 1962. The following year, a second trail with a Stabil Disc lift was added on the north face. It could accommodate nine hundred skiers an hour. The Birdseye Mountain Ski Center's directors also invested in snowmaking equipment, which was a relatively new concept at the time. This was a good idea because, as it turns out, that geographic area has one of the lowest yearly snowfall totals in the state, averaging only sixty to seventy inches. During the first year, there was no need to make snow because Birdseye Mountain was blessed with a higher-than-normal amount of snowfall. Based on this anomaly, in 1965, the directors decided to expand with a higher trail above the power lines, and added a Doppelmayr T-bar lift. Unfortunately, they vetoed the expense of additional snowmaking machines. The next two winters reverted to normal, low snowfall, and the ski center closed. The directors were unable to obtain additional funding from area banks to keep it afloat, and it didn't help that, at the same time, Killington Ski Area was being developed and competing for funds.

Bill Jenkins originally had innovative plans for the site, including building a Vermont theme park that would be called Vermont Mountain Park to showcase the state's history and culture. There was also talk of building a revolving restaurant on the mountain top. None of these plans came to fruition, however.

After the demise of the ski business, Birdseye Mountain was converted to a campground, with the addition of a swimming pool and other amenities. The former base lodge became the camper center. Don Sevigny and his father managed the 187 campsites, all of which had electric hookups and free firewood. The Sevigny family lived at the campground during the season and were available to help campers at any time. Many campers returned yearly, creating a relaxed, family atmosphere. The campground was in existence for about a decade. During the next twenty years, the trails and

Birdseye Mountain Ski Center, circa 1960s. *Courtesy of Bill Jenkins.*

campsites became overgrown, the empty swimming pool filled in with debris and the base lodge was destroyed in a fire. The current owner is developing the property's trails for use by all-terrain vehicles. The future of Birdseye Mountain as a recreational site is uncertain, but Don Sevigny believes it would not be too difficult to reestablish a beginner's slope with lights for night skiing and snowmaking equipment.

Today, one of the largest manufacturers in Castleton is Hubbardton Forge, which produces high-quality, wrought-iron lighting fixtures. The factory currently employs 184 people at its plant, which is located just south of Castleton Corners. Like many successful businesses, Hubbardton Forge had a modest beginning. The two original founders, Reed Hampton and George Chandler, both happened to take a studio art class at the University of Vermont from renowned sculptor and artist Paul Aschenbach. He recognized their talent and offered them a sort of unofficial apprenticeship at his own forge. Upon graduation from University of Vermont, they formed Hubbardton Forge and Woodworking and located their forge in an abandoned nineteenth-century barn in Hubbardton, Vermont, that had belonged to George Chandler's great-great-uncle. Before they could get things operating, they had to clean out mice, bat, snakes and numerous loads of cow manure.

The two young entrepreneurs soon recognized that there was a lot of competition in the woodworking end of their business, so they decided to specialize in metalworking; the name became simply Hubbardton Forge. In 1976, they produced their first line of candlesticks, fireplace screens and accessories. Sales started slowly until they advertised in *Yankee* and *Colonial Home* magazines. They realized there was a need in consumer markets for high-end wrought-iron lighting fixtures when the *Country Loft* catalog in Boston requested that they produce a lamp and then ordered one thousand of them. As the consumer market discovered that Hubbardton Forge offered quality workmanship and style, the owners found they needed additional employees. By 1988, the business had outgrown the old barn in Hubbardton, and they built a modern facility on Route 30, south of Castleton Corners. In the mid-1990s, Hubbardton Forge leased a showroom at the Dallas Market Center, achieving nationwide recognition; orders poured in from retailers around the country, from as far away as Seattle, Washington.

Hubbardton Forge uses a variety of machinery in production, from state-of-the-art to vintage. Its signature caged-basket design featured on lamps and other fixtures is fashioned on a wood lathe turned by an old tractor wheel George Chandler had found in the barn. The term "wrought iron" today refers to the process of a steel or low-carbon steel pipe being heated in a forge to make it malleable for shaping. According to Reed Hampton, " Metal is very plastic, and the French word for forging is *plastique*." Old-fashioned, foot-operated triphammer machines from the late 1800s are still used. These are more efficient than the hand hammering done by blacksmiths in bygone eras. The company organizes its workers into teams of fifteen and promotes a cooperative, collegial work environment. Quality control is a high priority. Work orders are color-coded, with colors changed daily to ensure that the first order on the floor is the first order to go. Every part and process is checked twice for consistency. In a typical day, Hubbardton Forge can produce 800 to 900 lamps and ships 700 to 1,200 pieces daily, filling at least two shipping company trailers and several trucks.

In recent years, Hubbardton Forge has continued to grow and provide employment in the area. It received the 5x5x5 Growth Award three years

Signature cage basket design lamp in progress at Hubbardton Forge. *Courtesy of Hubbardton Forge.*

in a row from *Vermont Business Magazine*, which recognizes the state's fastest-growing companies in five categories. In 2004, Hubbardton Forge was named Vermont's Outstanding Business of the Year, and George Chandler received the American Society of Furniture Designers' Pinnacle Award for lighting design.

Chapter 3
THE CASTLETON SLATE INDUSTRY

The slate belt of western Vermont, some forty miles in length, extends from Lake Bomoseen and Castleton south to West Pawlet and west to Granville, New York. This slate belt is part of the ancient Taconic Mountain range. About 500 million years ago, the region was covered by a tropical sea with a soft clay sedimentary bottom. Around 375 million years ago, the sea floor was thrust above sea level. Tremendous heat and pressure transformed the sediment into a metamorphic rock called slate. During the uplift process, the oldest layers of rock were pushed toward the surface, so that the Taconic Mountains have upside-down layers, with the oldest at the top.

The chemicals present in the clay cause the color variation of slate. Red slate contains hematite that is combined with iron oxide. This red slate can only be found around Granville, New York. Rutland County slate was formed during the Cambrian period and contains either chlorine, which produces a green color, or hematite, which causes a purple hue. The complicated mix of elements determines whether green or purple slate will fade when exposed to air or fade very little, such as the "unfading green" slate from the Scotch Hill area of Fair Haven, Vermont. Much of the western Vermont slate is free of silex, or foreign matter, so it was in demand for a variety of industrial uses, such as switchboards.

Before the first slate quarries were dug, the area around Lake Bomoseen included a number of hill farms cleared for grazing cattle or sheep. The

Example of exposed sindine (uplift) at Glen Lake. *Courtesy of the author.*

first sawmills were built in the early 1800s. The logs cleared from pasture land were floated down Lake Bomoseen to the mill in Hydeville. A few years later, in 1839, Caleb Ranney and Colonel Alanson Allen started the first area slate quarry on Scotch Hill near Fair Haven. The slate was used for headstones, hearths and paving stones. By 1848, slate began to be used as roofing material, but Colonel Allen first had to prove to local residents that a building would not collapse under the weight of a slate roof. He persuaded a local man to allow him to put a slate roof on his barn, but the man stipulated that he would not pay for it for one year. If the barn was still standing in a year's time, Colonel Allen would get his money. The barn remained standing well into the mid-twentieth century, so it can be assumed Colonel Allen received what he was due.

In 1852, Boston financiers, headed by Newell Sturtevant, formed the West Castleton Railway and Slate Company. They acquired title to six hundred acres of land between Screwdriver Pond (now Glen Lake) and Lake Bomoseen on the west side of the lake. The site contained slate deposits and also had the advantage of a stream that dropped ninety feet, providing necessary water power to run a mill. The company constructed a narrow-gauge railway to haul the slate from the quarry and mills to the wharf on Lake Bomoseen. Three or four loaded cars at a time were placed on a barge powered by four horses on a treadmill. The barge delivered the slate-filled cars to the southeast corner of Lake Bomoseen, where they were then taken to finishing mills in Hydeville. In its first year alone, four thousand square slate roofing tiles were sent to the Boston market. By 1854, about 250 men were employed by the slate company, and small cottages were built to house workers and their families. By the end of the 1800s, the West Castleton community had over thirty of these cottages for the mostly Irish-Catholic immigrants who worked in the quarries and mills. Workers put in ten-hour days and were paid less than two dollars per day. The community could boast a school, several barns, two sawmills and a company store that also contained the company office and a U.S. post office. Atop this building was a bell to signal the start and finish of the workers' day. Today, it is a private home, but the bell is still there. The company owned the workers' cottages, and they were paid in scrip, not cash, which could only be spent at the company store. The store prices were inflated, thus keeping the workers perpetually in debt. This system was typical of factories of the era.

West Castleton Slate Company store, which has a bell on top of it. *Courtesy of the author.*

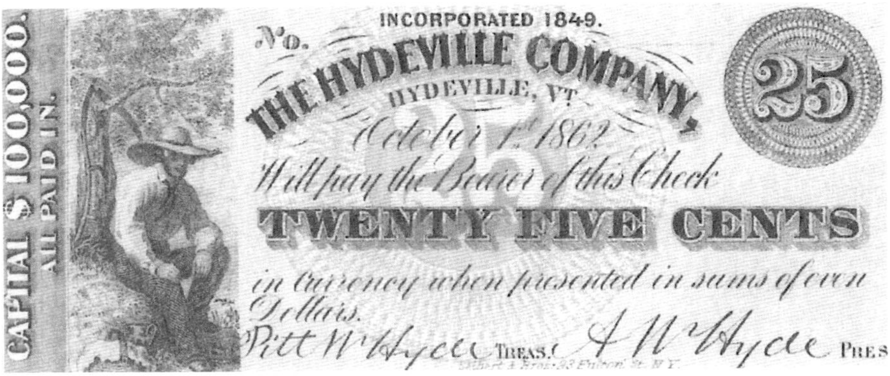

A Hydeville Slate Company scrip, with which workers were paid. *Courtesy of Danielle Woodard Budlong.*

In 1855, the number of employees dropped to 150, but around that time the West Castleton Slate Company developed the new process of marbleizing slate. This process mimicked more costly marble and made it possible for ordinary people to purchase items once reserved for the wealthy. The West Castleton Slate Company and others produced things such as one-of-a-kind mantels, clock cases, church altars, tabletops, game boards, kerosene lamp bases, bookends and pen-and-pencil sets. The new marbleized slate was much in demand throughout the second half of the nineteenth century. Partly due to the success of marbleized slate, the number of slate quarries in western Vermont continued to grow in spite of setbacks like fires and workers' strikes. By the early 1900s, the Vermont slate industry employed 1,300 workers and had sixty-seven quarries with fifty-eight operators. Ed Ryan of Hydeville, Vermont, owns a fine example of a marbleized slate fireplace. Fireplaces like his were often just made for show, more like a piece of furniture, and not used for warmth. The cost of a marbleized slate mantel at the time it was made was around $125, compared to $500 for a similar marble mantel.

Ryland Hanger brought the process of slate marbleization to Vermont from England in the mid-1800s. However, it had originated in Asia centuries before and was used in both Japan and China. In Vermont, the process became a closely guarded secret. The work was done by a small, select group of skilled workers, who often did the marbleizing at night after the regular employees had left for the day. Unfortunately, this secrecy at the Vermont slate factories

Ed Ryan's marbleized fireplace. *Courtesy of the author.*

led to the process being lost. The color formulas were kept locked in steel safes, but none have survived. The general process was as follows:

Local slate companies such as John Jones Slate Company of Castleton, O'Day Brothers, Penrhyn and Mahar Brothers of Hydeville delivered slate cut to specifications to the marbleizing shops. The work area was equipped with a tub or vat measuring twelve feet by four feet and ten inches deep that was filled about three-quarters full with water for the dipping process. At either end of the tub was a movable gate that regulated the size and density of the pattern. Prior to dipping, the slab of slate was rubbed smooth and given a base coat of paint. Next, it was baked in an oven overnight. The next day, paint of the desired colors was floated on the water in the tub and then gently stirred with a wooden stick to create the desired vein size and density. The movable gates also were used to create a ripple effect. Smaller pieces of slate were dipped by hand, face down onto the paint-swirled surface at an oblique angle. Larger pieces were lowered by use of a tackle system hung over the tub. Upon completion of dipping, the slate pieces were placed on

Sketch from *Slate History Trail* booklet, which shows marbleization process. *Sketch enhanced by Mary Trombley. Courtesy of Conservation Education.*

racks in the coal-fired oven and baked at a high temperature overnight. The cooled slate was sealed with varnish and baked again. The varnished slate was rubbed and received another coat of varnish, baked a third time and finally hand polished.

The high quality and reasonable cost of the marbleized items produced by West Castleton and other area companies helped the industry expand, providing increased employment in the area. The advent of the railroad in the mid-1800s allowed Castleton–area slate producers to ship their slate products beyond local markets. Vermont marbleized slate could be found in the Midwest in places such as St. Louis and Hannibal, Missouri. In 1855, the West Castleton Slate Company's display of marbleized slate items was a popular exhibit at the Vermont State Fair in Rutland, and it was awarded an unusually high prize of fifteen dollars. Later, thirty of its pieces were on display at New York's Crystal Palace and were lost when it burned down. In 1860, Castleton was the chief slate center in the area with 192 slate workers, followed by Fair Haven, Granville and Poultney.

With the end of the Victorian era, at the turn of the twentieth century, the demand for marbleized slate declined sharply. With the decrease in demand went the knowledge and skill needed for the process, so marbleizing became a lost art. Reportedly, the last person familiar with the complete process died in the 1950s. It seems unlikely to ever be revived, given the lengthy and time-consuming process, which would probably be cost-prohibitive today. However, fine examples of marbleized slate fireplaces, tables and mantels can still be found in older homes and buildings around western Vermont and nearby New York state, as well as at the Slate Valley Museum in Granville.

On September 1, 1868, it was reported that "the West Castleton Slate Company is erecting an immense mill for their business. It is over 300 feet long, 50 feet wide…In the future they will be able to fill orders promptly by reason of improved and enlarged facilities." A water wheel twenty-four feet in diameter supplied power from Hazard Brook.

Many of the early western Vermont slate companies had a precarious existence, due to financial setbacks, fires and other problems. Just three years after the new mill was erected, the West Castleton Slate Company became a victim to a disastrous fire in 1871 that destroyed the mill and several other buildings, with a loss estimated at $150,000. In 1875, it was reported that the company, once the area's largest employer, had been sold, but it was never reopened; it disappeared from sight. Interested visitors can take a self-guided tour of what

Remains of West Castleton Slate Company's mill that was built in 1868. *Courtesy of the author.*

was once West Castleton with a brochure that describes what was there. Several of the original slate cottages have been preserved as private homes.

The Western Vermont Slate Company began in 1850, and its property included almost a mile of Lake Bomoseen frontage, quarries, dwellings, a slate mill and other buildings. In the 1850s, the company was operated by H.E. Cook, and the little community that grew up around the slate business became known as Cookville, which was located on the west side of Lake Bomoseen between Hydeville and West Castleton. It had its own school, and a company store provided for the workers' needs. In 1869, the Western Vermont Slate Company changed hands due to foreclosure. The quality of slate had declined, and the business faltered. A fire in 1873 destroyed the mill. People left Cookville to seek work elsewhere, and the little village fell into disrepair. The Western Vermont Slate Company property was bought in 1887 by resort owner Horace B. Ellis.

The Hydeville Slate Company came into existence in the 1850s. It was acquired in the early 1900s by Penrhyn Slate Company, and its Cedar Mountain quarry, north of West Castleton, produced prized purple slate from the 1850s until around 1932. The Hydeville Slate Company took first place for its marbleized tabletops and mantels at the Rutland County Fair in 1859. Slate workers had a hard job. A typical Cedar Mountain quarry worker's day began with the 7:00 a.m. whistle and ended nine hours later at 4:00 p.m. Workers drilled holes into the slate ridge and inserted black powder to blast the slate loose. The usable pieces were brought to the mill for finishing, but 75 percent of the blasted slate was waste. The waste slate was moved by a runner trolley on a cable attached to a pole, called "the big stick." It was operated at first by steam and later with electricity. The constant loud crashes of the waste slate being tipped down the mountain became a familiar sound to area residents. Coulman Westcott records in more detail:

> *A narrow gauge railroad with push flatcars ran up to the mining pit. They were cable-looped together through a top pulley whereby as one filled car came down, it pulled an empty back up. At the bottom the track ran into the finishing shop where the slate was sawed and planed. The finished slate was then carted out to the quarry harbor where a boom crane lifted it into a large barge.*

The barge was towed five miles south to mills in Hydeville, where it was further finished and shipped by rail to distant locations. One wooden barge that never made it to Hydeville still rests in twenty to thirty-five feet of water off Cedar Point, reportedly carrying its load of slate. At the end of their workday, the slate workers rode the barge to Hydeville, where many continued on by trolley to their homes in Fair Haven or Rutland. Creek Road at the time was often impassable due to mud, earth slides or high water. Today, all that remains of the Cedar Mountain operation is a gigantic waste heap, resembling an extinct volcano. Anyone daring or athletic enough to climb to the top is rewarded with a splendid view of Lake Bomoseen and surrounding countryside. Cedar Mountain operated until 1932, and the machinery was disassembled in 1937.

In the 1880s, Samuel Hazard Jr. was supervisor of the Lake Shore Slate Company, with a new mill and quarries in West Castleton. The mill contained seven circular saws, a band saw, a jigsaw, five planers, two rubbing beds and a joiner, all powered by Little Hazard Brook. In the 1950s, Samuel's great-great-granddaughter, Martha Warren, left three hundred acres of the former slate company property to the State of Vermont for a game preserve. It is now the site of the Lake Bomoseen State Park, where summer visitors enjoy camping, picnicking, boating and swimming every year.

A Cedar Mountain quarry in the early 1900s. *Courtesy of John Durfee.*

The nature of quarry work made it both physically demanding and dangerous. Rock walls or loose pieces of slate could come crashing down with little warning, killing or injuring anyone in their path. Working with black powder was also risky, and numerous injuries or deaths were caused in blasting accidents. There were no such things as insurance or workers' compensation. Usually a collection would be taken for an injured or deceased man's family to help with expenses. Besides injuries caused by accidents, the quarry workers often had a poor diet; they also suffered from job-related respiratory problems. The pay for putting in nine hours of hard, dangerous labor was about twenty cents an hour in the 1880s, and even by 1916 most slate workers made only thirty to thirty-nine cents an hour. Periodically, the workers did try to organize at various quarries, and in the early 1900s, workers attempted several strikes. In addition to long hours and low pay, quarrying was largely seasonal work, from late spring through fall. Slate could not be quarried in the winter. When water seeps into the cracks, the constant freezing and thawing causes the slate to splinter, rendering it unusable.

Many slate quarries still operate in western Vermont and nearby New York State. They produce a variety of slate products from floor tiles to decorative items. For a more comprehensive history of the slate industry in the area, interested readers can visit the Slate Valley Museum in Granville, New York.

Chapter 4
OTHER SLATE-RELATED AND STONE BUSINESSES

The Slate Pencil Industry

1843–1872

An early slate industry along Lake Bomoseen in Castleton had its origin in a lucky discovery. In 1842, eighteen-year-old John Cain was fishing in Sucker Brook, which flows into Lake Bomoseen, and needed to weight his fishing line with a piece of stone. He broke up a larger rock and noticed it left marks on other rocks. He brought several samples of this softer rock back to West Rutland in his saddlebags, recognizing that his find might have some potential use. He whittled the rock into oblong, pencil-shaped pieces and marketed them to area schools for use as slate pencils. Local schoolteachers and their students found Cain's slate pencils superior to the imported German ones currently in use. The enterprising young man in 1843 purchased land from Hiram Johnson in a large ravine along Sucker Brook for the sum of $1,500 and established his pencil mill, a very modest one-man operation. Where Cain received the capital to start his business is not known, but it remained in operation for ten years, although it was never very profitable.

In 1853, Benjamin Adams and his son James, both of Castleton, bought out John Cain and started the Adams Manufacturing Co., with the goal

The American Slate Company pencil works on Sucker Brook. *Courtesy of Castleton State College.*

of eventually mass-producing slate pencils. They began on a small scale, much like their predecessor, but in the 1860s, they expanded—acquiring more partners and additional land—and built a factory. The new company was called Vermont Slate and Alum, possibly in hopes that if the slate pencil business petered out, they could still remain viable through mining alum. Incidentally, the material used for slate pencil manufacture was a type of softer slate that contained magnesia, not soapstone, as many people suppose. Soapstone was not hard enough to be cut into slender slate pencils.

The slate company dammed Sucker Brook to provide water power and built a paddle wheel. Later a forty-horsepower steam engine powered the mill, according to the Industrial Census Report of 1867. The mill site, along the western side of Sucker Brook (also referred to as "Pencil Brook") had five buildings, including living quarters for the workers, in its heyday. The mill itself consisted of a long five-room structure with a large, exterior, thirty-foot brick chimney, which was said to have contained a staircase. The slate first went to the sawing table, where it was cut into quarter-inch-thick slabs by one of four machines called a "shavy." The smaller slabs were then cut into pencils by the grooving machine. Next in the process was sharpening the slate pencils to a point, first done by hand and later by a machine. Finally, the pencils were sorted and packed into wooden boxes. They were taken by wagon to Castleton to be shipped by rail to more distant markets.

In spite of the use of machines to do much of the work, it took many workers to produce the slate pencils. At peak production, one hundred Irish immigrants working twelve-hour days, six days a week, could produce up to 100,000 slate pencils a day. Child labor laws were not yet in force, so whole families, including young children, worked at the mill. Housing for the unmarried men and smaller families was provided in a barrackslike building called a "Long Sue." This two-story building had double and single rooms, and measured 100 feet long by 20 feet wide. The foundation of another long building has been found, and it was even larger—125 by 50 feet—and had a massive slate foundation. Its exact use is unknown, but it has been speculated that it may have been a warehouse or barn.

By the end of the Civil War, the Castleton slate pencil industry was starting to wane. First, the local company was beginning to find increasing competition from less-expensive foreign companies. Also, by then, better-quality and less-costly paper was becoming available. Modern wood and graphite pencils quickly replaced the slate ones, and people preferred the portability of paper and wooden pencils over slate. The Adams Manufacturing Co. tried to hold on for a few years, even changing its name to American Slate Company, an appeal to patriotism over foreign products. Like so many flourishing businesses in the nineteenth century, it became a victim to progress as the new century and its advances approached. Slate pencils soon joined the buggy whip as obsolete curiosities. The Vermont Slate and Alum Company went into foreclosure in 1878, and court documents mention a burned pencil mill. Today, few remnants of the former pencil mill can be found amid dense overgrowth along Sucker Brook on what is today called Pencil Mill Road.

Using Waste Slate

As mentioned previously, the many uses of slate produced a great deal of waste, much of which can still be seen in huge slag heaps around the area. Well over 70 percent of the slate quarried ended up as waste. Vermonters, living up to their legendary New England thriftiness, began to wonder if there was some use for this waste. As early as 1912, a North Poultney man, "Hook" Hall, who was nicknamed due to his artificial hand, got the idea to grind red and green waste slate into a powder to be used as a paint filler. The red slate came from nearby Hampton, New York, and the green was obtained in Vermont. Hall's enterprise must have been successful enough because, in 1914, the Staso Milling Company, based in Massachusetts, bought him out. Staso got its name by combining the first letters of the three owners' surnames: Stanwood, Shu and O'Brien. The Staso Milling Company built a factory south of the village of Castleton and was the first to make widespread commercial use of slate waste material by developing a process in which slate was ground into granules. The slate granules were used in roofing shingles, early rubber phonograph records and the production of linoleum and asphalt. In 1919, the company was purchased by the Central Commercial Co. of Chicago, but they kept the name Staso. In an attempt to secure a steady supply of nonfading green slate, the Staso Milling Company eventually purchased all of Lone Pine Mountain, which consists of slate. This enabled expansion of their production—and expand they did. The company built a huge system of elevators and aerial tramways, conveyors, crushers, rollers, kilns and so forth. It must have resembled a giant Erector Set. The plant was only about half a mile from the Delaware and Hudson Railroad, so transporting their products posed little problem and greatly increased rail freight traffic.

Staso Milling Company in operation, circa 1920s. *Courtesy of Mary Beth Hadeka.*

Castleton would not be the same peaceful rural village for years to come. Its tranquility was soon broken with nerve-shattering regularity by blasting on the mountain, with the din of the machines crushing, grinding and pulverizing the slate and the racket of freight trains banging day and night. Noise was not the only problem. Houses shook, windows rattled and dishes fell off shelves during the blasting. The quarrying left an ugly scar on the mountainside; fine dust settled on everything. "At shift's end the clothes, faces, hands, hair, eyebrows and eyelashes of the men were a ghastly gray-green from the stuff." Strange appearance aside, the dust was corrosive and caused a variety of respiratory problems among the workers, including asthma, bronchitis, emphysema and silicosis. Years of lung irritation caused scar tissue to form in the lungs, and the resulting gradual decrease of oxygen could lead to death. In spite of the health risks, the pay was good and helped overcome most fears about health, as the following story from Jerome Towers illustrates:

> *An old fellow working in one of the dustier areas met an acquaintance "downtown" whom he hadn't seen in some time. Asked the friend, "Workin' Ted?" "Ay-uh," replied Ted. "Where?" the friend asked. "Up to the Staso Mill," answered Ted. "Ain't that a purty dusty place?" inquired the friend. "We-e-l-l," said Ted, proudly. "Mebbe. But they ain't no dust on them paychecks."*

Staso became the largest user of explosives in New England when it converted to the well-drill method of blasting during the mid-1930s. A well-drill machine bore holes six inches in diameter, up to three hundred feet deep and about eight feet back from the quarry rim. This machine worked night and day. The holes were filled with explosives under the direction of an explosives expert from the DuPont Company, and the usual blast used 20,000 pounds of dynamite. The charges were fired electronically. Needless to say, the resulting shocks of these repeated and immense blasts took their toll on village houses, particularly those along South Street. People filed lawsuits for structural damage. During court proceedings in one case, a seismograph—normally used to record earthquakes—was set up on the lawn of one area couple who claimed the blasting had caused their kitchen floor to collapse into the basement, taking the young wife, who'd been baking a cake at the time, with it. She survived, fortunately, but the cake did not. Most of the suits were settled out of court, and the company eventually reduced the amount of explosives used.

For an industry that began ostensibly to use waste slate, the Staso Milling Company soon began to have problems with its own waste products. In an effort to cut down on dust, the waste was sprayed with water, which created sludge. By 1917, it had covered several acres and was oozing toward South Street. So the company built a system of dikes to contain it. In time, a good-sized pond of wastewater formed, with the slate sludge on the bottom. It provided a good ice-skating surface for area residents in the winter, and bullheads could be fished from it in the summer, although swimming was not to be recommended, as the stirred-up bottom soon turned the pond into a soupy, grayish mess. The sludge field eventually covered some forty to fifty acres, but today it is overgrown with trees and brush.

During the late 1920s, home builders began demanding different colors for their shingles, so Staso developed a wider color range. After World War II, business and production boomed when a new off-white shade was developed for the Sunbelt markets. As time went on, Staso saw more competition from roofing companies closer to the source of pigments. The final blow arrived in 1958, when the Minnesota Mining and Manufacturing Company purchased land in California to build a new roofing mill. The Fry Roofing Company, Staso's largest customer and supplier of roofing to Sears Roebuck, canceled their orders with Staso. The employees were informed the plant would close at the end of 1959, leaving about two hundred workers unemployed.

In spite of the problems the slate company created for the community, Castleton reaped benefits as well. The company provided employment not only for hundreds of workers, both locally and from as far away as Oklahoma, but side businesses grew up as a result. Many elderly widows or women with disabled husbands opened rooming houses for the workers or took them in as boarders. There was no public restaurant in the village prior to World War II, so local women also provided meals for hungry quarry workers. It brought revenue to the railroad as well; Staso was the second-largest shipper on the Delaware and Hudson Railroad, after the Schenectady, New York General Electric plant. And finally, the Town of Castleton missed the tax revenue generated by Staso after it ceased operations in 1959. Today, only a few large storage bins and remains of concrete buildings exist, and the quarry is nearly full of water. Lone Pine Mountain still bears a scar where tons of slate was blasted away during the Staso years.

After Staso closed, during the 1960s and early 1970s, the Plastic Crete Company operated in the Staso location, but the oil embargo during the 1970s forced the company into bankruptcy. In 1974, twin brothers Jerry and Billy Hadeka, recent UVM graduates who had worked in their father Adolph's slate quarry in Hampton, New York, decided to purchase the old Staso site when it came up for auction. They had the idea of crushing waste slate for landscape and other uses. It took the family five years to clean out the site and salvage anything useable. Today, Jerry and his wife, Mary Beth, run Hadeka Stone Corporation. His brother Billy and his wife, Dale, are also owners; Bill is the quarry supervisor for the family's red-slate quarry in Hampton, New York. Their older brother, Ray, handles sales for both the Staso Road—known as the "green Staso" because it produces green slate—and the Hampton "red Staso" locations. Hadeka produces a variety of stone products, including Northeast Fast Dry, a compound used for surfaces on tennis courts because it is durable but not hard on players' feet and legs. It also provides materials for baseball fields, and several years ago, the company did a women's softball field at Middlebury College. The story of the Hadekas' vision, hard work and resulting success illustrates how the story of slate use in Castleton has evolved from modest beginnings through environmentally unfriendly practices typical of industry in the late nineteenth and early twentieth centuries to a modern company that has reclaimed and cleaned up an eyesore and made it viable and attractive.

In addition to Hadeka Stone Corporation, there are several other thriving slate and stone businesses in Castleton today: RMG Stone Products Inc.; Vermont Marble, Granite, Slate, and Soapstone Co.; and Camara Slate Products, Inc. Camara Slate is a family-owned business that specializes in architectural, flooring and roofing slate. Brown's Quarried Slate Products, Inc. produces naturally colored crushed slate for landscaping and other uses. RMG Stone Products, owned by Dave Socinski, is located on East Hubbardton Road in Castleton and produces a variety of slate and stone products, including monuments, landscaping and building materials, slate flooring and outdoor items such as garden benches and bird baths. Its slate countertops were featured on an episode of the DIY Network's Kitchen Renovation series. Vermont Marble, Granite, Slate and Soapstone Company is owned by Paul Thompson and has been located on Route 4A, just east of Castleton Corners, for four years. The company manufactures countertops, sinks, cookware, gift items, woodstoves, masonry heaters and monuments. It promotes its product line through the Internet, YouTube and Livestream Video. These modern companies continue the more than century-old tradition of Vermont stone working to provide beautiful and practical items for the twenty-first century.

Chapter 5
CASTLETON'S COUNTRY STORES

Castleton has witnessed an astonishing variety of stores come and go over the years. Many of the earlier stores in the village were destroyed by fire during the early twentieth century, so little or no trace of them remains today. However, a few early stores still exist, in one form or another.

In Hydeville, several families in succession owned a store located on the south side of present-day Route 4. It was variously called the Kelley Store, the O'Day Store and Quinn's Store. Today, it is a two-family home.

One of two country stores in Hydeville today is the Harborview General Store, currently owned by Dave and Pat Finlayson. The building originally housed the horse stable for the Hydeville Inn. It was later converted by contractor John Kenworthy into a beauty salon, Red Barn Coiffures, for Kathleen Mulligan. Her father, John Mulligan, ran the Hydeville Inn at the time. Since the 1970s, the building has been a country store, owned in turn by seven different owners.

Kevin and Laurie Knauer owned it the longest to date, about 20 years. They opened July 1, 1980, on an auspiciously sunny day. They called their business the Bomoseen Harbor General Store and Red Barn. On their first day of business, Kevin found himself breaking up a potential brawl right outside the store. A man came running in and asked to use the phone. Shortly afterward, the parking area began to fill with trucks, and two groups of men were squaring off. Kevin brandished an ax handle and yelled at

RED BARN COIFFURES

For The Look That Counts

Personalized **High Styling** — Shaping & Permanent Waving
Enjoy coloring under our new COLOR MACHINE that does ALL coloring in one-tenth the normal time.

FREE Consultation — Stop in and see us soon

HOURS:

Tues., Wed., Sat., 9 a.m. — 6 p.m.
Thurs. and Fri., 9 a.m. — 9 p.m.
No appointment necessary Tues. and Wed.
Closed Monday

Located on Rt. 4 Behind Lake Bomoseen Inn
Hydeville, Vt., Phone 265-4222

This page: An advertisement for Red Barn Coiffures, and a photo of Bomoseen Harbor General Store during Knauers' ownership. *Courtesy of Castleton State College and the author.*

them to take their trouble across the road, hoping to head off this showdown at the OK corral. The police arrived and broke it up before the fight got beyond the name-calling stage. It turned out that one group had been hired to tow vehicles away from the park in Fair Haven, where they'd been left, and their owners were protesting mightily about being towed! In spite of this dramatic—or possibly traumatic—event, the opening was successful. They sold their entire first order of beer, fifteen hundred dollars' worth, within a few days and ordered a second shipment. They tried to keep their prices low, and they were willing to accommodate their customers' needs by staying open until 11:00 p.m. On one occasion, they opened at 4:00 a.m. so a hunter who needed ammunition could get a good jump on the start of hunting season.

Kay Bronson, a longtime employee, "came with the store," according to Laurie. Kay's husband, Lloyd Bronson Sr., had had a boat business on the lake outlet for many years, and she knew everybody. A lot of regular customers came in to chat with Kay, and she often worked evenings, which allowed the Knauers to relax on the deck of their living quarters above the store. One evening they looked out to see a boat on a trailer rolling backward down Creek Road toward Route 4A with a man in pursuit. He managed to catch his runaway boat and trailer before any mishap occurred.

The Bomoseen Harbor General Store and Red Barn was a true old-fashioned country store with a little bit of everything, from deli foods to basic grocery items, newspapers, fishing tackle, clothing such as T-shirts and boots and firearms and ammo for area hunters. If they didn't have something a customer needed, they'd get it the next day. The Knauers maintained a dock on the lake outlet for customers who wanted to come by boat. (Author's note: His children fondly recall going there by boat with their grandfather to pick out candy.) Kevin also had the job of regulating the dam at the end of the outlet for the State of Vermont. He let out water when necessary to keep the lake level within three inches of normal depth. Today, the dam is computer-operated by the state. Kevin fought an ongoing battle with a colony of beavers for a while. When he'd let out water, the beavers would fell more trees to stop the flow. Kevin would remove the logs, and the beavers would start all over again. Families often fished from the dock or near the dam, and Kevin and Laurie made a point to take a picture of any child who caught a fish. These pictures went up on a wall in the store, and often years later, the "kids" would come back and point out their fish pictures to friends or even spouses.

During the Knauers' years of ownership, they saw changes in their customer base that reflected different times. During the summer season, a large percentage of customers were summer renters, who came for two-week vacations and bought their groceries and other needs. In the early 1980s, Vermont still had "blue laws" that didn't allow larger stores, like the Grand Union in Fair Haven, to be open on Sundays, but smaller establishments were exempt. This especially helped beer sales at the Bomoseen Harbor General Store. Over the course of a summer, some of the cottages had as many as ten different families renting. As time went on, fewer rentals existed; new owners remodeled their cottages for use as personal summer homes, so the turnover slowed down. Once the summer people left, the college students returned, and to some extent, they made up for lost summer business. When the drinking age was still eighteen, students would come over to the Bomoseen Harbor General Store to get something to eat after a night out at "the Dog," (the Hydeville Inn). This unusual nickname for the Hydeville Inn created a humorous misunderstanding. One day, Kevin's father, who was not a local man, was filling in at the counter. Someone came in and asked where the Dog was. He directed the person upstairs, where the Knauers' pet dog was kept, not realizing the customer was looking for the bar!

Kevin and Laurie eventually bought the Bronson home behind the Bomoseen Harbor General Store and rented out the apartment over the store. A large number of children got on the school bus in front of the store in those days. Their own two children would eat breakfast at the store before catching the school bus, and after school, they stopped for a snack. The Knauers hired many high school and college students during their years of ownership, and many have kept in touch with them. Although they no longer own the store, they still live in the same house.

In October 2000, Mary Doran became the owner. She had grown up in the area and was part of a large family, but she had been working in other parts of the country. During a visit home, she learned the store was for sale and purchased it. She upgraded its appearance and merchandise, adding items such as gift baskets, Green Mountain coffee, homemade grinders, baked goods and local products. After a year, she sold it to Stan Yablonski, who had it for a year or so before the current owners, Dave and Pat Finlayson, took it on in 2003.

The Finlaysons have built upon what Mary Doran started, with an attractive variety of country-style gifts, cards, Lake Bomoseen shirts, Vermont products, Pat's homemade muffins and other baked goods, sandwiches, basic grocery and snack foods, newspapers and a coffee bar featuring ten different varieties of Green Mountain coffee, available hot or iced. During the summer season, their famous Creemees, which is soft ice cream, are served from an outside window. Each week a different special flavor is featured, such as maple or black raspberry, along with either chocolate or vanilla. A sure indicator that the summer season has started is the appearance of the Creemee flavor-of-the-week sign on the side of the building. The Finlaysons also added a beverage section and large cooler across the back of the store. They cater to local and seasonal residents, outdoor enthusiasts and both summer and winter fishermen.

The other Hydeville store is Mrs. T's Country Store, which is located just across the intersection of Creek Road and Route 4A. The small building has been home to several previous businesses, including Hutchins Fuel and a Dart Mart gas station. Today, it is owned by Carol A. Thomson, who acquired it in November 2007. When Mrs. Thomson bought the business, it had been a convenience store run by Orson Kingsley for about two years. She gave the store a new coat of paint but otherwise kept it much the same. The store sells typical convenience store items: beer, soda, and snack foods. Mrs. T's also sells nonethanol gas, which is preferred for boat and lawn mower engines. The store is patronized by both local people and summer residents, along with sportsmen during the fall and winter hunting and ice-fishing seasons.

During the early twentieth century, Williams Store was located on Creek Road, just south of the Point of Pines cottage community. This store was unique in that it was one of the few commercial establishments on Lake Bomoseen that was accessible by both road and boat. The two-level store had an ice cream parlor on the upper story, and at the lower level, it rented boats and sold bait. Many a family around the lake has fond memories of going there to get an ice cream cone. Today, the former store has been converted into a private home that is owned by Paul and Marsha Fontaine.

Heading east on Route 4A from Hydeville and Creek Road is one of the larger area markets, now called Prunier's Market. It originated in 1963, when Russ Norton and Ken Bonner erected a two-pump Chevron gas station on an empty lot. When the two-bay garage was completed, Norton did repair and body work. While the garage was under construction, Norton began selling potatoes from a little shed next to the site. He realized a good profit could be made selling vegetables, so eventually he converted the garage into a store. He didn't completely get out of the auto-repair business, however, as he added a small garage behind the store so he could still tinker with cars. He also added a slate-topped private bar in the back where he entertained friends.

The summer season was very busy, and Russ Norton employed as many as fourteen full- and part-time employees. This was before the Route 4 superhighway existed, and people didn't drive to Rutland as often for their needs. Norton allowed families to shop on credit and pay on a monthly basis. Norton's Store employed a full-time meat cutter and gained a local reputation for good-quality meat. The store was neat and clean and retained a quaint charm. Some people thought Russ Norton had "the Midas touch" because he had success with whatever he tried. He had no interest in selling or leasing the store until he was diagnosed with lupus in 1968, and he became too ill to keep up with it. Just prior to that, he had actually been planning to purchase land south of Route 4A to build a mobile home park. Due to his illness, he leased the store to Albert Pelletier and eventually sold the business to Lee O'Donnell.

The Charles Prunier family purchased the former Norton Store in 1976. The Pruniers have been in central Vermont for at least three generations. Frank Prunier ran a slate quarry on Scotch Hill just north of Fair Haven, which is where his son Charlie grew up. Charlie's wife, Marjorie, came from

Norton's Gas Station, with potatoes for sale in background, in 1954. *Courtesy of Joan Brown.*

Prunier's Market today. *Courtesy of the author.*

Claremont, New Hampshire. Their three sons, Charles Jr., Bill and Dave, run the store today. Prunier's Market still serves local and summer customers, saving them time and gas needed to drive to Fair Haven or Rutland to shop. Besides a full selection of canned and frozen foods, bakery items, deli and quality meats, a popular feature at Prunier's is the monthly Pizzarama, with made-to-order pizzas that customers can take home to bake. Prunier's also makes sandwiches and offers a selection of prepared meal items at the deli department. In 1998, local contractor John Lord remodeled the store. Prunier's still sells gasoline like the original business started by Russ Norton, but it has no service station.

Continuing east on Route 4A, the next store is Beverage King. It was started by Pat Bruno in 1982 and was originally called Beer King II. Bruno already owned a Beer King in Rutland. Prior to being a beverage store, the building originally was built by George Pritchard as a garage. At one time, it housed truck and motorcycle repair businesses. After four years, Pat Bruno sold the business to Bernie and Connie Woodbury, who gave it the current name of Beverage King. The store changed hands again on September 27, 1994, when it was purchased by Joe Sessock. Since acquiring the Beverage

King, Sessock has made numerous improvements: the bottle redemption center has been enlarged; additional cooler space, an expanded wine room with a large selection of wines and a deli counter that does a brisk takeout sandwich business were added; and in addition to beer, wine and soda, the store also stocks newspapers, milk, bread and snacks. Plans for the immediate future include razing an old house that stands in front of Beverage King to provide additional parking and direct access to the store.

During the 1930s, MacRae Orchard's apple stand was located on the corner of Drake Road and Route 4A. It was so busy on weekends that cars were parked on both sides of 4A. In the late 1940s, Josephine Rice operated a sandwich shop there. The property was sold in the summer of 1950 to Roscoe and Sylvia Nesto, who opened Nesto's Market. Mel Patch worked there for four years and said it was where local people bought their meat, as Coon's Store not carry fresh meat. Nesto's sold groceries, vegetables and a complete line of meats. In the back, there were a walk-in cooler, refrigerated case and the meat saw. In 1965, Beverly Davidson and Connie Gibbs bought the store and operated it until 1987. The building is still there, but it now contains two apartments.

A recent addition to the Castleton Corners business community is technically neither a country store nor a restaurant, but the Heilsamr Bakery, located at the back of the parking lot of the Bomoseen post office, deserves mention because it fills a need in the community. Owned by Bonnie and John Ennis, the bakery opened on August 1, 2009. It embodies Bonnie's dream to have her own bakery, using the recipes handed down by her German grandmother. The bakery's name comes from the German word meaning "wholesome." On any given day the bakery is open, you can follow your nose through the door and find Bonnie making breads, pies, cakes and cookies. The Ennises have tried to involve the local community for equipment and supplies while establishing the business. The clientele consists of senior citizens, local people—many of whom stop daily for a goodie on their way to work—college students, summer residents and visitors passing through. The summer season between Memorial Day and Labor Day, along with the holidays, are its busiest times. When it gets very hectic, sometimes customers pitch in to help, which reaffirms Bonnie's belief that "there is still goodness in humanity."

The Castleton Corners Deli and Citgo Station is on the former site of the nineteenth-century Sargents' Plow Manufacturing, on the corner of Routes

4A and 30. During the 1930s, it was an Amoco gas station and was eventually sold to Bill Kelly. It next passed to John and Gail Bruno. Gail Bruno was instrumental in converting the repair station into a country store that today not only fills customers' vehicles at the pumps but also satisfies their appetites with coffee, doughnuts and other baked goods and deli sandwiches. On May 1, 1996, the Brunos sold the business to Lorraine and Tim Keller.

The current owners redesigned the deli, doubling the original space, and in 2003, they tripled its size. In recent years, Castleton State College students have voted the Castleton Corners Deli as "the best in the state" for its warm, homemade muffins and cookies and for the fresh submarine sandwiches. The clientele is largely local working people, but business swells during the summer season, when summer residents and visitors return to the area. The hardworking, friendly staff treats customers like friends, and discussions about everything from the weather to local news can be overheard. Like most small-business owners, Tim and Lorraine can relate many humorous stories involving customers. In one case, a regular customer came to fill up his truck, put the nozzle in and disappeared. The store staff looked everywhere, but they couldn't find him. So they finished filling the vehicle and pushed it off to the side. About an hour later, he reappeared, explaining he'd gone to see about a job and simply forgot about his truck!

Another loyal customer was not allowed any sweets. However, once in a while, he'd slip in for an ice cream sandwich. One day as he was enjoying his forbidden treat, Tim spotted the man's wife. He sent him scurrying to the back and out through the bottle room to avoid detection. Tim says, "We have a group of characters in the store. Some are so funny no one would believe it. Many times we think Hollywood should make a sitcom about us. America would roar with laughter." He also added that he feels they are blessed by their friends, and they have witnessed many acts of kindness. In his opinion, "People are basically very good."

On the opposite corner from the Castleton Corners Deli is the site of one of the area's earliest stores, Coon's Store, a fixture for lake area residents for many years. It also once housed the Bomoseen post office until the present building was erected. Lewis and Ida Mae Coon came to Castleton Corners in 1888 from Putnam, New York, with their young son, Clarence. In 1889, they bought the store and an acre of land for $1,550. The store filled a need for area residents and summer visitors alike, and it did very well in its first two years of operation. However, Lewis invested in a slate business that failed and forced him into bankruptcy in 1901. Fortunately for the family, Ida Mae was able to buy the store at public auction. From then on, the property was in her name, and she kept her hand in the business.

Coon's Store was open from 7:00 a.m. until 9:00 p.m., seven days a week, making it the only store in town open in the evening. In 1914, the post office was moved from the Lake House when that establishment was sold, and Clarence Coon became postmaster. The Bomoseen post office had no postal delivery in those days, and it was not especially busy until the hotels sent out bulk advertising and summer residents arrived.

Coon's Store stocked a variety of bulk staples such as crackers, coffee beans, cookies, tea, flour and sugar. Salted cod was sold in one-pound wooden boxes, and pickles and salt pork were sold from barrels. Many area homes and camps relied upon oil stoves, so kerosene was available for five cents a gallon. It was a typical general store, with everything from hardware to penny candy and Schrafft's chocolates by the pound. Dry goods like cloth and sewing supplies kept local seamstresses happy. Bananas and magazines hung from hooks over the display cases. The store did not sell fresh meat—only hot dogs and bologna—because local butchers delivered meat to their customers, but it had the cheese wheels that are a hallmark of general stores. Clarence Coon later became interested in radios. He was

Coon's Store, circa early 1900s. *Courtesy of Mel Patch.*

one of the first in the area to sell and repair radios, mainly Atwater Kent and Crosley. Clarence kept a radio at the post office where patrons could listen to it, a good advertisement for the ones he sold.

It may surprise readers to learn that buying on credit is not unique to modern-day credit cards. It was common practice for households to charge their purchases by running a tab and then pay off their bill weekly or every two weeks, depending on how the breadwinner was paid. Summer people often did not settle their bill until the end of the season. Coon's Store offered an incentive to pay up promptly: when a man paid his bill in full, he was given a package of cigarettes. If a woman paid the bill, she received a half pound of chocolates.

While no mail was delivered from the Bomoseen post office at Coon's Store, groceries were. Local boys picked up orders around the lake by bicycle. Crates of filled grocery orders, as well as two or five gallon cans of kerosene, were delivered by truck. The kerosene cans, plugged with a potato, were put in racks on the side of the truck to avoid food contamination.

Coon's Store became a gathering place for the local community. During the day, women came in to shop, pick up mail and chat. In the afternoon when school let out, children were clustered at the penny candy counter. In the evening, men came in to buy tobacco and pass the time with acquaintances,

Front view of Coon's Store and the Bomoseen post office. *Courtesy of Linda Splatt.*

discussing crops or town politics while enjoying a smoke. It was rare to see a woman in the store at that time of day.

In the summer of 1917, Coon's Store was the scene of a crime that gave the townspeople plenty to talk about. During the night, burglars broke through a rear window and blew the door off the safe in the post office with nitroglycerin, leading to speculation that they were professional safe crackers. The explosion woke the Coon family, who raised an alarm, and the robbers took off with about seven hundred dollars. They left before seizing the store's cash box, and they were traced as far as Lake Champlain and Ticonderoga, where they evidently escaped across the lake.

Clarence Coon owned the old Westover Hotel on the northeast corner across from the store, but he did not operate it as a hotel. For a time, they had an ice cream parlor, run by hired girls, on the ground floor. Clarence also had a display room for his radios. They rented apartments upstairs, and the barn out back was used for storage. An interesting side note is that two buildings just west of Coon's Store were owned by the power company and were known as "the humming station," as alternating current was changed into direct current there to run the trolley line.

Coon's Store remained in the family until 1959, when Lewis Coon's grandson, Clarence Oakman, sold it to Davidson family. The Davidsons sold it to David

The Westover Hotel and trolley coming down from Lake Bomoseen. *Courtesy of the author.*

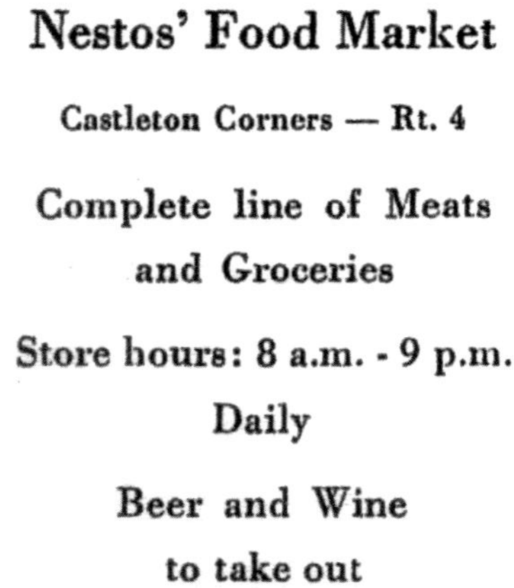

Advertisements for Prunier's, Nesto's and Coon's Store. *Courtesy of Castleton State College.*

Murray, who continued to operate the store until the 1990s. In its last years, the store was known for selling Ben and Jerry's ice cream "seconds" at a reduced price and continued to sell the usual items like newspapers and grocery staples. Today, the building still stands, but it houses a Coldwell Banker realty.

A short distance north on Route 30 is the Jiffy Mart, another convenience store. It sells gasoline, beverages, newspapers and food items, like most country stores. It started out in the 1970s as a motorcycle and snowmobile shop. Since then, it has been an arcade and a Subaru dealership before its present incarnation. John Smiel is the current owner.

Continuing farther north on Route 30, in 1967, Taggart Brothers Construction built a store for George Merkel on the site of the former Town Farm. Merkel's Store catered to local residents, summer people and, during the academic year, Castleton State College students. In the winter, the store was also patronized by out-of-state ski associations. Merkel's Store sold groceries, homemade bread, pastries and pies, deli items, pizza, beverages, fishing and hunting supplies and newspapers. In 1973, the store was robbed, and George Merkel Sr. pursued the thieves by car all the way to Poultney, where he ran out of gas. His son had borrowed the car the night before and had not refueled it.

At the north end of the lake on Route 30 is the Lake Bomoseen Campground, owned and operated by Daniel Sr. and Estelle Adams. They purchased it in 1984 from Rod Holzworth. It has been in existence since 1955. Besides sites to accommodate every type of camping, from tents to RVs, Lake Bomoseen Campground has a country store. Campers can purchase recreational supplies and basic camping necessities, snacks, beverages, souvenirs gifts and books. The Adamses maintain a family-oriented facility, and many families have been returning for twenty years.

Returning south again on Route 30, heading back through Castleton Corners toward Poultney, you will come to Brown's Roadside Market. It has been in business for one hundred years, although not continuously at its present location, which dates to 1974. It began when Charlie Brown Sr. loaded his horse and wagon with fresh vegetables grown on the family farm and went from door to door, selling his produce to customers as far away as Whitehall, New York. It was hard work tending and harvesting the vegetables and then delivering them far and wide, but Charlie persevered at this business until the 1930s, when advances in refrigeration and competition from stores no longer made home deliveries economically worthwhile. Charlie Brown recalls his grandfather telling that when he'd deliver vegetables to Alexander Woollcott on Neshobe Island during the 1930s, they'd shout "new man on island!" to alert Woollcott's eccentric and famous guests to be clothed—for some, clothing was optional!

The original Brown's Roadside Market was located across from the present-day Tag's Motel on Route 4A. From the last Saturday in June through the week before Thanksgiving, Charlie Brown Sr.'s wife, Annie, could be found running the stand. She only closed up half a day for Governor's Day at the Vermont State Fair in Rutland. The whole family went to enjoy the fair, and a highlight was seeing the vegetables at the 4-H building.

The Brown family's produce was renowned for its freshness. Charlie Sr. picked ripe tomatoes and cucumbers twice daily. When sweet corn was ready, it was picked four times a day. After dinner Charlie and Annie harvested beets and carrots, which were kept cool overnight in the cellar. Each day, any unsold corn was fed to the pigs and cows. Their granddaughter, Darlene, remembers as a child she and some friends would hide in the corn patch and sneak out to pick cucumbers. They'd slip back in the corn rows and enjoy their pilfered snack with a little salt. Charlie always seemed to know a few of his cucumbers were missing!

In 1926, Charlie Brown Sr. relocated the stand just east of Castleton Corners, as it was more convenient to the farm, and "the Corners" had more traffic. At the new location Annie decided to expand their selection beyond what was grown on the farm, so they began ordering fruit from a man named Mr. Harsberg in Albany. Annie was very particular about the quality. If one peach had a bad spot, she'd reject the whole basket. Maple products, candy and soda were also added to the stand's product line.

Apples and fresh-pressed cider became a mainstay and a major attraction for customers at Brown's Roadside Market. The apples were pressed into cider at a mill in Blissville, Vermont, and later at other mills, until they acquired their own in 1975. The cider was sold in glass jugs that Charlie purchased from the Coca-Cola Company. It was the children's job to clean and label the bottles, which had once contained soda syrup. They were paid a penny a bottle. Customers returned their bottles to be refilled from a fifty-gallon barrel. The only drawback to this practice was that honeybees were attracted to the sweet cider, and if one got into the bottle during refilling, they would have to overflow it to remove the bee. Today, the Brown family still presses its own sweet cider that contains no preservatives. The label still has the slogan created by Annie: "Pa Brown Says: If you want this cider old, bear in mind to keep it cold. If you're out to make it hard, sot [*sic*] it right in the sunny yard. But, if you really want a drink that's neat, take the darn stuff when it's sweet."

Over the years, the Browns' stand has developed a loyal customer base that often goes back generations, not only due to the freshness and quality

Brown's Roadside Market, on Route 4A, in 1948. *Courtesy of Elizabeth Patch Wilkinson.*

of the produce, but also because of their policy of honesty and their belief that the customer is always right. One time a woman returned a five-cent cucumber, claiming it wasn't fresh. She was given a replacement, even though Annie knew that cucumber had been picked only hours before. Busy as she was, Annie always had time to chat and exchange news with her customers, and the succeeding generations have continued this friendly tradition. The family often socialized when work was done at "kitchen hops" with their neighbors. They'd gather at one another's homes and dance in the kitchen.

The former location of the Browns' stand on Route 4A in Castleton Corners still exists. When it was still open, entering the building was like stepping into the past. A calendar from 1929 hung on the wall, an original Coca-Cola cooler filled with water kept the soda bottles chilled, and Annie tallied up the bill on an early National cash register. In 1954, the Browns added a back storage room and a cellar to keep the produce cool and dry. When Annie Brown passed away in 1969, the cash register quit working, but it was recently repaired. By the 1970s, Brown's Roadside Market found it harder to compete. The increased mobility and competition from larger stores and the

Brown's Roadside Market today on Route 30. *Courtesy of the author.*

decline of the large hotels and children's camps on Lake Bomoseen that had provided steady patronage for many years had an adverse affect on business. Annie Brown's son, Robert C., took over the stand after she passed away, and in 1978, Robert's son, Charlie, succeeded him. It closed for two years, until Robert Brown's daughter, Darlene, reopened it in 1984.

Today, the family continues to provide fresh produce, local Vermont products such as syrup and honey, seasonal items and homemade baked goods, including the pies for which Mary Brown, Charlie's wife, is deservedly famous. The busiest time of year continues to be summer into fall, when sweet corn comes into season and locally grown apples and the new crop of cider attract customers. Before Halloween, local children come to select potential jack-o'-lanterns from a large variety of pumpkins, set amid a backdrop of fall decor and scarecrows. The addition of a heating system has allowed the stand to remain open year-round, selling Christmas trees and wreaths in addition to their other products. The Browns attend local fairs and farmers' markets, as well as the Vermont State Fair, to display their products. Charlie is now into his thirty-second season at the Rutland Farmers' Market. They credit their continued success to local and seasonal customers who return for the quality of the produce, the friendly service and the diversification. Charlie sold his cows in 2000; he now sells topsoil in the spring, and his son runs the family slate quarry. They grow thirty-two acres of sweet corn, four acres of pumpkins and produce sixteen thousand gallons of sweet cider a year. Charlie carries on a family tradition of hard work and perseverance that goes back numerous generations, when the first Charles Brown lived in Castleton during the Revolutionary War period.

The Great Depression may have seemed an unlikely time to start a new business venture, but in 1935, George H. Eddy did just that. He opened a grocery store in the village of Castleton, located on Main Street where the Laundromat is today. Mr. Eddy used a $3,000 loan from the Rutland Grocery Company, where he ordered his groceries, to purchase the store. In spite of the hard times, he was able to repay the loan within two years. During the Great Depression, farmers brought their produce and farm products to the store, and George Eddy paid them the market price. In turn, the farmers bought their staples—such as flour, canned goods and meat—from him. George Eddy's business flourished through home delivery of meat and groceries to the surrounding community and to summer residents along Lake Bomoseen. Eventually, he employed six people and had two delivery trucks. Betty Zahnleiter worked there in the late 1940s to early 1950s while her husband was in law school. She recalls packing box after box with groceries for the delivery trucks going out to Lake Bomoseen.

Staples such as flour, sugar, coffee and tea were purchased in bulk, and the store typically sold several twenty-five pound bags of flour weekly. Coffee beans were ground at the store, and customers could ask for special blends of the bulk teas in stock. Everything was fresh, as there was a rapid turnover. Customers remained loyal to Eddy's Market not only for the quality of the products and free delivery, but also because Eddy's was generous in extending credit. Of course, like most country stores, Eddy's Market also served as a social hub, where people ran into friends and neighbors and traded news. The store was remodeled in 1935, 1939 and again in 1970 in an effort to keep up with customer needs and expectations.

The gas rationing and scarcity of workers during World War II put an end to the delivery business. After the war, lifestyles began to change, and people started driving to Rutland to do their shopping. The customer base had changed as well. The older, longtime customers were dying. During the 1970s, Eddy's Market saw a new type of clientele; with the continued expansion of Castleton State College, its students, who often did not have cars at that time, frequented Eddy's for their needs. Accordingly, Eddy's accommodated them with an increased selection of snack foods, soda, beer, wine and cigarettes. Eddy's also cashed checks for the students, which was a real convenience in a village that didn't always have a bank within easy walking distance. By adapting to changing needs and times, Eddy's Market remained in business for over forty years. Finally, though, the family found competition from larger grocery chains too hard to keep up with, and they decided to give up the business.

Besides Eddy's Market, three other grocery stores existed at one time or another in the village of Castleton. Of those, only one remains: the Castleton Village Store. Prior to its present incarnation, the same building housed Ballard's Store in half of the ground floor. The other half contained a post office and Bill Hart's insurance office. The present-day Castleton Village Store has reclaimed those two spaces. In the former Ballard's Store section, on the left side, one can still see where the original soda fountain stools were once fastened. Prior to being owned by Mr. Ballard, the store was owned by Mr. Wright. He sold everything from paint to student supplies needed by Castleton State College students. Mr. Ballard worked for Mr. Wright and eventually bought him out. Artifacts from these two former owners can be seen displayed on shelves on either side of the Castleton Village Store, including the original Ballard's Store sign. Many local people, as well as college students needing part-time jobs, worked at the former Ballard's Store; among them were Frances Gray and Eileen Colburn. They remember there were milking machines in the back.

An amazing variety of items were sold in Ballard's Store: Pittsburgh Paint, guns and ammunition, drug sundries, greeting cards, camping, fishing and bathing (swimming) supplies and ice cream by the cone or gallon, in addition to the usual grocery store staples. It truly was one-stop shopping for local residents, almost a mini-Walmart!

In the early 1970s, Ballard's Store was purchased by Keith Jennison, who had returned to Vermont after serving as a combat correspondent for the War Department and completing a stint as a book editor. Jennison added a sizable book department to the store. His ownership was rather short-lived, as in 1973, he sold it to John and Pam Rehlen, who still own it today. Jennison got out of the grocery business because he had been offered a position as a journalism professor at Castleton State College.

Castleton Village Store today. *Courtesy of the author.*

Since the Rehlens acquired the store, they have made many changes and improvements, but they have retained the old-fashioned charm of bygone years. The store occupies the entire ground floor of the building, and they added coolers for beer and soda; an addition was built in 1980. They also have a large selection of fine wines. Besides canned goods, snacks, beverages and other grocery staples, the Castleton Village Store sells newspapers and magazines, greeting cards, gift items and books by local authors, including Pam Rehlen herself. The Rehlens feature many local Vermont products, from baked goods to Castleton Crackers, Green Mountain coffee, maple syrup, cheese and Vermont-raised gourmet meats. The store itself does not have a deli counter, but a related business just across the side parking lot makes pizza and deli sandwiches. The Castleton Village Store serves nearby Castleton State College students during the academic year, as well as local people and summer residents. The Rehlens have continued to hire college students as part-time employees.

Chapter 6

THE MANY INCARNATIONS OF ROUTE 4A EATERIES

As the saying goes, "You gotta eat," and an astonishing number of restaurants, snack bars, diners and other variations of eating establishments have been in existence over the years along Route 4A in Castleton. Many of the early eateries have passed into history, but a number remain with changes in name, ownership and appearance.

The Lakeview Restaurant was just off Route 4A, a mile and a half north on Creek Road and along the west shore of Lake Bomoseen. Mortimer and Janet Brown owned this establishment from the summer of 1963 until the fall of 1966. Customers drove up Creek Road to the restaurant, located just south of the boat launch, or came by boat and docked at the Lakeview. It had a kitchen capable of preparing meals for fifty patrons at a time, a forty-foot dining room and a cocktail lounge. In good weather, patrons could be seated on the spacious porch that provided a pleasant setting with its view of the lake. The Lakeview was managed by the very capable Kendall Ladd, who also managed the Wobbly Barn near Killington. Tom Harris was the cook, a graduate of a culinary academy. One of his popular specialties was filet mignon with mushroom caps. The Lakeview Restaurant also promoted holidays such as Father's Day with special meals. Two waitresses served customers, one inside and one for the porch. Weekends were very busy, and during dinner hours, a local organist played the Hammond organ.

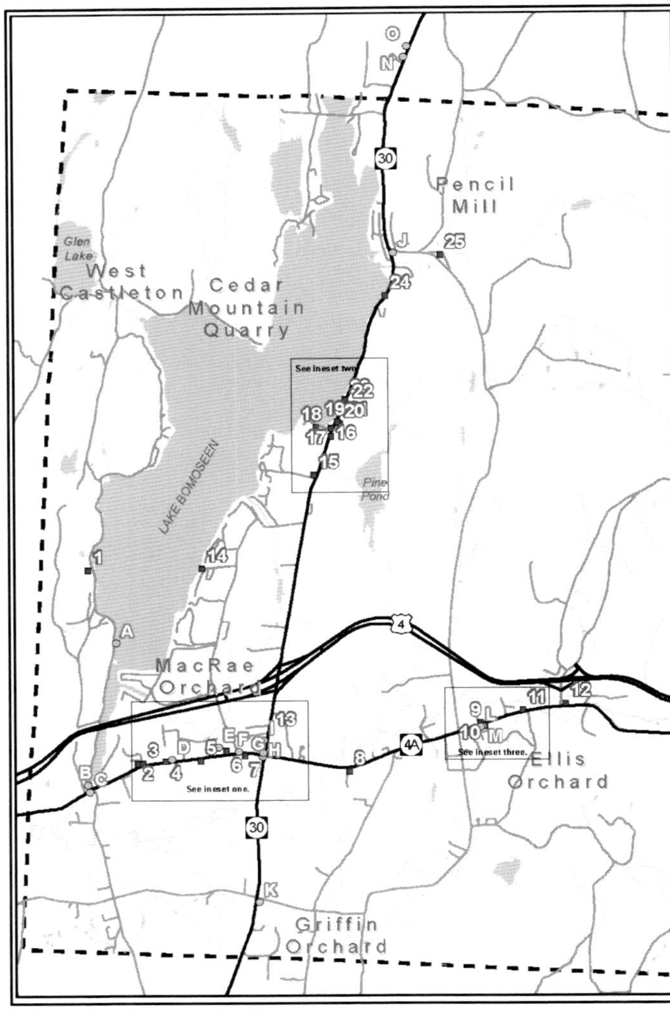

Map showing locations of Route 4A and Route 30 eateries. *Courtesy of Steve Schild of the Rutland Regional Planning Commission.*

There have been several different restaurants located near the present-day Hydeville Plaza on Route 4A. In May 1941, the owners of the Birdseye Diner in Castleton advertised the opening of the Birdseye Drive-In in Hydeville, where the plaza is now. It was under the same management as the diner, and it advertised booth, counter and curb service. The menu included the most popular sandwiches from the Birdseye Diner. Very few people remember the actual drive-in, however. George and Charlie Looker

The Location of Restaurants and Country Stores in the Town of Castleton, Vermont

Restaurants

Name	Code
Lakeview Restaurant	1
Patrizias / Stray Cat / Cinco Gringos	2
Paul's Family Pizza	3
The Coffee Cup	4
The B&B Diner	5
Wells CreeMee Stand / Iron Lantern	6
Roxies	7
The Castleton Snack Bar	8
Birdseye Diner	9
The Blue Cat Bistro	10
Green Mt. Country Depot	11
Fort Warren Restaurant	12
Sunrise Family Restaurant	13
Pioneer Lodge	14
Pine Cliff Lodge / Trak II	15
Eddies	16
The Gate House	17
The Country Club	18
Calvi's Grill	19
Trak - In	20
Frank's Place	21
Ringquist	22
Somewhere II / Cedar Grove Lounge	23
Uncle Charlies / Lakehouse Bar and Grill	24
Crystal Ledge / The Stables	25

Country Stores

Name	Code
William's Store	A
Red Barn / Harbor View General Store	B
Hutchins / Dart Mart / Mrs. T's	C
Norton's Store / Prunier's Market	D
The Beverage King	E
Nesto's Market	F
Coon's Country Store	G
Castleton Corners Deli	H
Jiffy Mart	I
Merkel's Country Store	J
Brown's Roadside Market	K
Eddie's Market	L
Ballard's Store / Castleton Village Store	M
Bomoseen Camp Ground	N
Pumpkin Patch Country Store	O

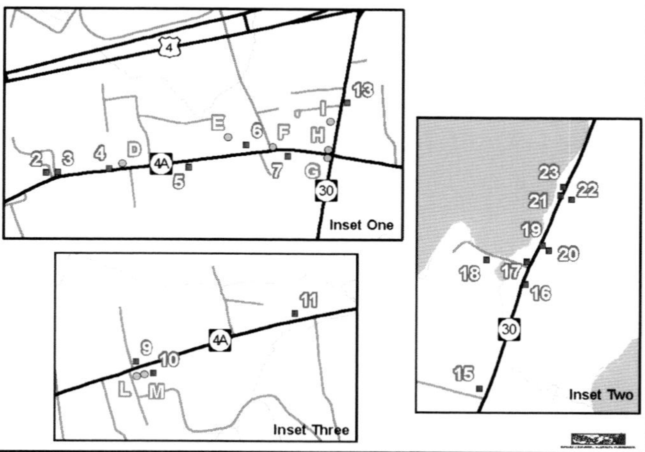

were ahead of their time with the concept of a drive-in, but with the sudden involvement of the United States in World War II and subsequent gas rationing, it did not last long. It probably was not economically feasible to try to maintain two establishments.

Just across the parking lot from the Hydeville Plaza is Paul's Family Pizza. The building containing the pizzeria began quite differently, however. It originally was part of the Bunny Rabbit Motel, a nicely landscaped

Advertisement for Patricia's Restaurant in Hydeville in the *Rutland Herald* on June 18, 1976. *Courtesy of Castleton State College.*

Advertisement for Birdseye Diner and Drive-In. *Courtesy of Castleton State College.*

1950s motel complex owned by the Phillips family. The motel was easily recognizable due to its large, wooden rabbit sign out front. The motel units were eventually torn down, but the building that now houses Paul's remained. Several other businesses occupied the premises, including Dr. Ashcroft's chiropractic office. Paul and Judy Wiskoski started the pizza business on June 22, 1991, largely at the urging of their daughter, Alaina. At the time, she was the only one in the family with experience in making pizzas. Prior to then, Paul had been a plumber, and Judy worked as an ambulance attendant. After a period of trial and error of creating their own sauce and dough recipes, the Wiskoskis became successful largely by being consistent and carefully weighing and measuring the ingredients. Paul says, "The pizza you get today will be the same pizza if you were to buy it tomorrow." Phil Mallette has managed the shop since 1991. He is in charge of preparing everything in the morning, six days a week. Customers of all kinds, especially hungry college students on tight budgets, enjoy the Tuesday special of $5.00 cheese pizzas. The pizzeria has added some homemade dessert items to the menu recently, and it also has Ben and Jerry's ice cream treats available. June 22, 2010, marked the nineteenth anniversary of the business.

In 1974, Patricia and Buddy Taggart opened a small restaurant on the north end of the Hydeville Plaza, called Patricia's Restaurant. Soon Buddy built a thirty- by sixty-foot addition with sliding doors so they could seat up to 250 people. Both the original facility and the addition had its own bar, so two separate groups could be accommodated. Patricia's offered live entertainment on Friday and Saturday evenings. The bandstand still exists on the premises today.

Patricia's advertised "fine food and spirits for gentlemen and their ladies." New England-style pot roast was one of the most popular specialties served. Pat Taggart recalls many loyal patrons came in every weekend and always sat in the same spots. Pat worked in the kitchen, and Babe Roussin, a locally renowned baker, made the breads and pies. Marie Quinlan was the hostess, dressed in a white uniform. Once as a wedding reception was about to begin, Pat's son Mark brought in a roast beef to be served. His mother told him to slam the meat down on the spiked serving board. He took her too literally and splattered Marie's white outfit from head to toe with meat juice!

Patricia's Restaurant was open seven days a week, and the Taggarts never took a day off. In 1976, Pat wound up in the hospital, and the restaurant was sold after that. For less than a year, it was operated as the Stray Cat, which advertised live entertainment featuring the New Leaf Band. Then it became the Rusty Rail Bar. When that closed, two different pizza shops tried their luck in the smaller section of the former Patricia's before they, too, closed. That section of the plaza remained empty for five years. Now Moments to Memories, a scrapbook supply shop, occupies one part, and a new eatery, Cinco Gringos, a Mexican restaurant, recently opened on the other end. The two businesses are still separated by the sliding door, but today, shelving in the scrapbook shop hides it. The Taggarts' nephew, Bob Barnes, and his co-owners, Ed Pack and Michael Jakabes, remodeled the site, adding tile on the floor and kitchen walls. A family member decorated the walls with brightly painted murals to create some Mexican ambiance. Cinco Gringos opened on December 1, 2009, and has had a good start, drawing permanent and seasonal residents and college students.

Heading east on Route 4A, the next eatery in line was the Coffee Cup, a small diner run by Bill and Harriet Bowen. They were quiet, hardworking people, and they kept the diner open long hours. Bill always worked at the same slow but steady pace, and was nicknamed "Slow Bill." The little red restaurant had only four tables and about eight counter stools, a jukebox and a pinball machine. The Bowens also rented six to eight small tourist cabins behind the diner. Longtime summer resident Eugene "Fuzzy" Harris recalls driving up on Friday nights from Connecticut with his friend Bob Toner after the two had finished their shifts as policemen. They arrived late, at about

11:00 p.m., tired and starving. The Coffee Cup was one of the few places still open that late, so they'd pull in to get something to eat. Fuzzy relates how the older woman who did the cooking would make small hamburgers similar to today's popular "sliders," and they would always order several, telling her, "Don't stop making them now!" They enjoyed the burgers but swore off the coffee in favor of soda. By the time they got there, the coffee would have been stewing for hours and was so strong it was nearly undrinkable. One time Bob Toner's brother and son Kevin stayed at one of the cabins, which by then were not in the best of repair. They discovered the hard way that the roof leaked, and they shared the accommodation with a snake.

An unusual feature at the Coffee Cup was the custom of encouraging patrons to write poetry on paper scraps, paper napkins, matchbook covers or whatever else was handy. Jane Macomber Foley recalls that, as a teenager in the 1970s, "we would stop in for late-night dessert, especially pie and homemade brownies. The brownies were rich and chocolate-y, with fudge frosting. If you wrote a poem, it would get tacked up on the wall, and you would be rewarded with a free brownie." Eventually, the little restaurant became the home of John and Helen White, and it was later purchased by Bob and Caren Helm. Alan Woodard purchased the property and built a large post-and-beam home and barn on the site. No trace of the Coffee Cup remains.

A little farther east on Route 4A, near the current location of Gilmore Lumber, was a diner that was first known as Kehoes' Pine Diner, run by Ed and Ruth Kehoe during the 1940s. Elizabeth Patch Wilkinson worked weekends at the diner as a teenager and met her future husband there. Roy Wilkinson drove a truck for the Crystal Ice Company and made regular deliveries to the diner. When the other employees got wind of the budding romance between Elizabeth and Roy, they played "I'm in Love with a Wonderful Guy" over and over on the jukebox when he'd come in.

After the Kehoes, the diner was owned by Babe Roussin and was called the B&B Diner. The Bs referred to Babe and her husband, Butch. Babe had a well-deserved local reputation for her homemade breads and pies, which were a real draw. The B&B became very popular, so much so that the Roussins opened a second B&B on Route 22A that was north of Fair Haven. When the B&B closed, Babe Roussin became a pastry cook for Patricia's Restaurant in Hydeville and then at the Wheel Inn in Benson.

In the 1950s, Harry Wells opened a frozen custard stand on Route 4A, where the Iron Lantern Restaurant is located today. Harry's Cree Mee stand,

Kehoes' Pines Diner, circa 1948. *Courtesy of Elizabeth Patch Wilkinson.*

Cree Mee stand that was owned by Harry Wells on Route 4A. *Courtesy of Linda Splatt.*

constructed from a concession stand formerly at Crystal Beach, was located on the site of a former baseball field just west of Castleton Corners. In addition to frozen custard, the Cree Mee served snacks and light meals such as hamburgers, hot dogs and soda. The snack bar had no indoor seating, but customers could enjoy their frozen custard and hot dogs at picnic tables provided by Harry.

In 1967, the Cree Mee stand was sold to Jack and Ruth Helm, who already owned another similar establishment called Johnny's Snack Bar, which was located across from Paolino's Greenhouse in Fair Haven. The Helms remodeled and enlarged the former custard stand and called it Johnny's Restaurant. Jack's son, Bob Helm, and his wife, Caren, recalled that during 1967 and 1968 when the new Route 4 highway was being built, Jack fed the construction workers daily and allowed them to run a tab during the week and pay it off when they got their paychecks.

At the end of their first summer season, on August 25 through August 27, Jack and Ruth Helm featured a Johnny's Thank You special menu, with advertised specials such as a lobster roll for eighty-nine cents and a butterscotch sundae for just nine cents with each dinner order. They also announced they would remain open all winter, with a new heating system in place. Throughout the year, they had Sunday family buffets with themes such as German beer garden, Hawaiian luau or New England favorites, all with appropriate decor.

"Most Sundays there were at least one hundred people waiting in line for a table. The most famous and popular dishes on the buffet were Ruth Helm's homemade pies," her daughter-in-law Caren reminisced. In 1970, the Helms expanded, adding a larger dining room on the west end of the restaurant. They advertised a Thanksgiving buffet featuring roasted Vermont turkey; tender baked ham; vegetables, including corn on the cob, squash and asparagus; homemade bread; a relish tray; six different kinds of salad; and pumpkin or mince pie and beverage, all for $3.50! Children under twelve could eat for $1.75. Johnny's was so popular with local people and visitors alike that all of its parking lots would often be full, and the overflow parked along the shoulder of the road. The restaurant hosted various groups in the downstairs banquet room. One time, however, Jack committed the faux pas of serving individual, artificial creamers to a group of dairy farmers, and the co-op president jokingly called him on the carpet for it.

In 1976, Jack and Ruth Helm sold Johnny's Restaurant to Robert and Susan Stein, who renamed the place the Checkmate Restaurant. Robert

This page: Advertisement for a Hawaiian luau at Johnny's Restaurant in the *Rutland Herald* on August 11, 1972, and an aerial view of Johnny's Restaurant on Route 4A, circa 1960s. *Courtesy of Castleton State College and Mel Patch.*

Stein, "a former Navy man, was co-owner of a restaurant on the Killington access road called the Knights of the Round Table, and the new name for Johnny's was a spin-off from that," according to subsequent owner Joe Sessock. The Steins continued the tradition of serving good, home-cooked food at reasonable prices. They aimed to have "something for everyone," as an ad of the period declared. During the 1970s, a weekday lunch special was priced at $1.00 to $1.50, and a Mother's Day buffet was advertised for $3.95. Daily dinner specials of choices such as steak, spaghetti or a seafood combination with "seconds on us" were popular. Children ate at half price during the Saturday-night buffet. Those not wishing to come in and sit at a table could order at a takeout window. The Checkmate also had a lounge called the Knight Club, a clever play on words, which featured entertainment every Tuesday through Saturday evenings from 9:30 p.m. until closing. Eventually, a craft-and-gift shop was added on the west end of the restaurant, where the restaurant clientele could buy homemade fudge, Vermont crafts and collectibles.

The Checkmate was sold in 2000 to Joe and Susan Sessock, who currently own the Beverage King store in Bomoseen. Joe revamped much of the restaurant, making it more upscale, changed the menu and renamed it Main Street Pasta and Grille. He decorated the walls with local historical photos, a tradition that the current restaurant, the Iron Lantern, has continued. Unfortunately, it only stayed in business for nine months. Joe is the first to admit that they didn't really know a lot about the restaurant business at the time. The Sessocks leased the restaurant to David and Lisa Foster and their partners, Mike and Heather Rosen. These four became the owners in 2003 and still own it at the present time. The Iron Lantern is open for lunch and dinner and provides excellent dining in a relaxed, country ambiance. The current owners remodeled the kitchen and expanded and redecorated the lounge, which offers entertainment on Friday and Saturday nights. The Iron Lantern also offers wings and pizza for those wanting a casual takeout meal.

Another eatery located on Route 4A is Roxies. It is fairly new to its present location, but many people today don't realize the business has been in existence for many years. The original owner, Earle Wilson, had an amusement concession at Crystal Beach on Lake Bomoseen in the early 1940s. A World War I veteran, he spent some time on the carnival circuit before settling down to run his concession business. He called it Wil-Sonia, and it featured a Ferris wheel, penny arcade and a children's train

This page: Advertisement for Checkmate Restaurant and Craft Shoppe in the *Bomoseen Promoter*, and a look at what is now the Iron Lantern Restaurant. *Courtesy of Castleton State College and the author.*

ride. He began selling popcorn, French fries, peanuts and hot dogs from his food wagon, which he drove to Rutland's Main Street Park every day. He somehow acquired the name, "Roxie the Popcorn Man." No one is sure of the exact origin of the name, but the family believes it was a takeoff on the word "moxie," which means courage and spirit in the face of adversity. During World War II, food supplies became difficult to obtain, so the family purchased their popcorn and potatoes from local farmers, and they even made their own carbonated soft drinks. The whole family pitched in to help with the business, peeling and cutting potatoes for the French fries and making their own pickle relish.

Sandie Rivers is the current owner of Roxies. In 1957, her grandparents, Gertrude and Norval Ramson, took over Roxies, which became famous for its French fries. Roxies, a landmark for many years at the Vermont State Fair, has been in the same family for over fifty years. Gertrude, known as Gram to her family, was the spark plug behind the business. Sandie recalls her grandmother's generous spirit: "If someone dropped their ice cream cone or hot dog, Gram would always give them a free one." Gram Ramson was a hardworking, energetic and adventurous woman. She rode a motorcycle and was one of the first women in the area with a pilot's license. Gertrude's great-granddaughter, Amanda, recalled that Gram worked in the kitchen until she was eighty-six years old, and she had a hard time letting other family members take over.

Sandie started working at the stand at age thirteen, and today her daughter and granddaughter help with the business. In 2002, Sandie and her husband, Tony, purchased a long-term lease in Castleton Corners and set up a 280-foot concession trailer, in addition to the stand at the state fairgrounds. It is open from late spring through fall. Hungry customers can sit at the picnic tables provided or in their cars. The menu remains largely the same, with new items added from time to time. Roxies is known for their special flavor of soft ice cream: black raspberry. The owners have made improvements to the Route 4A site, such as a children's play area. With the addition of a football stadium at Castleton State College in 2009, Roxies now has the food concession there, so a new generation of young people can become familiar with this local institution. Sandie's dream is to build a permanent structure some day so that Roxies can remain open all year.

The Castleton Snack Bar on Route 4A, about a mile east of Castleton Corners, has been a fixture in the area for many years. It began its existence as part of a float on a flatbed trailer in the Rutland Dairy Parade, which was attended by President Dwight Eisenhower in June 1955. After the parade, John and Eileen Brough had it brought to its present location, and they used it to sell homemade soft ice cream. It changed hands numerous times after

Roxies Stand at Castleton Corners. *Courtesy of the author.*

the Broughs had it; some of the owners were Glen and Beatrice Erwin, Gordon Austin and family, Bud Hutchins, the Goodspeed family, Mike Duignan and finally John Wells and Myrna Wilkins.

The Austins bought the snack bar in 1958. They had little experience, as Gordon Sr. had had a milk route previously. Eileen Brough showed them the ropes, such as preparation of the various food items, including "Friday Hotdogs." These were two fish sticks tucked into a hot dog bun and were for Catholic patrons who could not eat meat on Fridays in those days. In 1959, an addition for a larger kitchen area was built, and the menu was expanded to include items such as hamburgers and French fries. During the Austin years, the snack bar became known for its six flavors of soft ice cream: chocolate, vanilla, strawberry, black raspberry, coffee and orange–pineapple. This last flavor was unusual, but it was so popular that fans came from as far away as Albany to get some. Its formula consisted of half a can of ice cream mix, three ounces of "high peak," three ounces of vanilla and the desired flavoring. The Austin children loved the ice cream too, and one day their mother complained to her husband, Gordon Sr., that the kids were eating too much of it. He wisely told her, "Let them eat all they want." Within a month, they had lost their appetite for ice cream! Over their ten years of ownership, the Austins learned that owning an eatery was a seven-day-a-week job, and that you were constantly working. Once the first mealtime rush passed, you had to get ready for the next. The Austins installed the familiar sign that still sits atop the snack bar. Originally, it was out by the road, but when they found people were throwing things at it, they moved it to the roof. The original sign was restored by subsequent owner John Wells after the neon lights no longer worked. An artist created the little mouse eating Swiss cheese; the cheese camouflages the holes where the lights once were. At first, the ice-cream-cone logo was removed, but people complained so much that it was put back on.

The current owners of the Castleton Snack Bar are John Wells and Myrna Wilkins, who purchased it in 1995. They have not changed the physical premises much, but they have expanded the menu to provide many more choices, such as homemade chili, pulled pork, homemade lemonade and iced tea and deep-fried mushrooms, onion rings and zucchini. They offer twenty-four flavors of soft-serve ice cream. John supports the local Little League with free ice cream cones after the games. They also remember the family pooch; they have doggie ice creams with dog bones. The popularity

Castleton Snack Bar on Route 4A. *Courtesy of the author.*

of the Castleton Snack Bar can be witnessed on any warm summer evening, with a line at the takeout window for ice cream or a quick meal.

A Castleton village institution is the Birdseye Diner on Main Street (Route 4A). In 1936, prior to World War II, Charles and George Looker opened the original diner, which was a small wooden building that burned in 1958. The original diner was open twenty-four hours and featured full-course meals. A photo survives of people celebrating V-J Day, the end of World War II, in front of the diner.

Over the years the Birdseye Diner has had at least eleven different owners and several different names. William and Norma Keane owned it the longest thus far, from 1952 to 1971. After the fire, it was called the Silk City Diner, then the College Diner, Jim's Diner and T.J.'s Diner, reflecting a progression of new owners. In 1960, the business moved into a sleek, stainless-steel and enamel 1950s-style diner. In 1996, John and Pam Rehlen acquired the diner and changed the name back to its original one, Birdseye Diner. They have restored it, inside and out, and expanded the dining area into the space formerly occupied by Castleton Discount Beverage. With this addition, they can now seat seventy people. On many weekends, the diner serves over four hundred people, so the new addition has proven beneficial. The west wall features a painted mural that depicts various Castleton historical landmarks.

Many of the Birdseye Diner's staff have been providing friendly service for ten years or more. Head waitress Debbie Griffin has been there for twelve years. Like most small-town diners, the Birdseye Diner has its regulars who come in daily for coffee or a meal and to chat with friends and neighbors. College students and their visiting families frequently gather for breakfast there as well. It is open for breakfast, lunch and dinner. In warm weather, people can eat outside at umbrella tables along the front of the diner. During Castleton's Tuesday evening Concert on the Green summer outdoor music series, many people grab a quick meal at the Birdseye before strolling down the street for the concert on the green next to the Federated Church.

The Blue Cat Bistro is one of Castleton's newest restaurants. It is owned by John, Pam and Wenger Rehlen and managed by Wenger Rehlen. The Blue Cat opened in 2007 and is located in the rear of the same building that contains the Castleton Pizza Place and Deli, next to the Castleton Village Store. The building formerly housed a truck service bay for Clayton White's Esso station. The Blue Cat specializes in a variety of pasta dishes, brick-fired pizza, salads, chicken and steak entrees and a good selection of wines and

This page: Celebrating the end of WWII in front of Birdseye Diner in Castleton, Vermont. Also, this is what the diner looks like today. *Courtesy of Castleton Historical Association and the author.*

beers in a relaxed and cozy setting. Patrons dine under a unique ceiling with a twinkling mural of the night sky. The management strives to keep the menu moderately priced while maintaining high-quality food with a gourmet touch. The Blue Cat offers Castleton village residents, college students and visitors another local dining alternative in addition to the Castleton Pizza Place and Deli and the Birdseye Diner.

The front part of the building that houses Blue Cat Bistro has been home to Castleton Pizza Place and Deli since 1988. It is owned by John and Pam Rehlen. It has a huge selection of sandwiches and wraps and variations of pizza. The restaurant is popular with college students, summer visitors and local residents all the time, but like the Birdseye Diner, business is especially brisk during the summer Tuesday evening Concert on the Green series. Many concert-goers order pizza or a sandwich to carry across the street and enjoy during the outdoor concert.

Heading toward West Rutland on Route 4A, a local landmark has been preserved, thanks to the dedication and determination of largely one resident, Mary Ann Jakubowksi. When the trains no longer stopped at Castleton, the 1850s-era depot was sold. Mary Ann's family purchased it, and it was used for several different purposes, including a player piano shop. After extensive restoration, the old depot has been returned to its former appearance inside and out, and a new business, Green Mountain Country Depot, occupies the east end. This bakery and deli serves sandwiches on a variety of breads baked on the premises; pastries such as cinnamon rolls, for which they have achieved well-deserved attention; cookies; muffins; and deli salads. They also offer barbecued chicken or pork on weekends, cooked outside on a sheet-metal grill that resembles an old locomotive. Customers can eat at several tables inside the charmingly restored depot, or in good weather, there are a few tables on a newly added, large deck behind the station. Kelly Draper and Lynn Kratochvil are the owners and bakers for the business. They previously operated a bakery in Poultney, Vermont. The Castleton depot has been reestablished as an official Amtrak train station, with two scheduled stops per day. This is a boon for Castleton State College, Middlebury College and Green Mountain College students, who travel from far away, and for local residents. For the past fifty-five years, the station was not in operation, so passengers had to go to Fair Haven or Rutland to take the train.

Just east of Castleton village, another eatery—the Fort Warren Restaurant—was located across Route 4A from the Fort Warren Drive In

This page: Green Mountain Country Depot, which is now a bakery and deli as well as a railroad station. *Courtesy of the author.*

theater. It was run by Barlow and Betty Rozell in 1967. In 1969, the restaurant was rented by John and Eileen Brough, and they ran it until John's death later that summer. It was later bought by the Dracziks. In the early 1970s, Robert and Caren Helm bought the property, sold off the restaurant equipment and used the building to house their Castleton Gardens and Florist business from 1972 to 1990. Today, the building is used for apartments.

Chapter 7
ROUTE 30 RESTAURANTS

There have been a number of eateries of one sort or another situated along Lake Bomoseen on Route 30 over the years. One that existed for about three decades was Pioneer Lodge. In 1922, Fred and Anna Maccabee owned property near the cottage community known as Little Rutland, located near the intersection of Drake Road and Route 30. At first, they lived in a tent on their land. After a lot of hard work, they built a restaurant called Pioneer Lodge. The Maccabees specialized in New England-style home cooking. On Sundays, a chicken dinner, billed as being "like Grandmother used to make," was a popular choice. Thursday nights featured a traditional New England boiled dinner. A humorous anecdote about Mrs. Maccabee was recounted in the August 6, 1944 issue of the *Resorter.* A man came in and asked for "crawlers." Mrs. Maccabee said she didn't have any, but she'd try to oblige and told him to come back the next day. She faithfully went out that night after dark, searching for night crawlers, but she had no success. When the man returned, she apologized and told him she hadn't been able to find any—there just weren't any out that night. The man looked at her oddly, but at that moment a woman came into the restaurant, asking for doughnuts. When she left, he said, "Why, that's what I wanted!" It seems the regional difference in what people call fried dough was to blame for the misunderstanding. He had wanted *crullers*, a kind of doughnut, and not fishing worms!

Pioneer Lodge

and Annex

Little Rutland • McRae Road

Directly on Lake Front Our 30th season catering to vacationists at Bomoseen with our own home cooked food and real old New England meals.

Tel. Fair Haven 224-W2

This page: A postcard of Pioneer Lodge and an advertisement. *Courtesy of the author and William Earls.*

In 1967, the Maccabee family sold the property to David and Agnes Earls. By that time, the building had not been used as a restaurant for many years, and it had been divided into three apartments. The Earls opened up the apartments and converted it back into a family summer home. In the mid-1990s, they tore down the old building and rebuilt a new, smaller year-round house on the site. They used the design of the original building to help determine what the new house would be like and even reused some of the original windows. The postcard of Pioneer Lodge shows a sign advertising ice cream for sale. Jim Leamy, a board member of the Lake Bomoseen Association, recalls as a boy he would go from the Lamphears' cottage on Green Bay to get ice cream at Pioneer Lodge. The Earls family still possesses a few reminders from the Pioneer Lodge era: a large brass bell that once hung under the eaves and could be rang by a rope from inside, an old sign post and the signatures of former Pioneer Lodge patrons scrawled on the wall of the garage basement.

Another restaurant on Route 30 began as Pine Cliff Stock Farm, located just north of where Bomoseen Golfland is located today. Owner J.K. Pine of Troy, New York, was a gentleman farmer who raised prize racehorses, sheep and cattle. During the second decade of the twentieth century, Pine Cliff Stock Farm could boast sixty Jersey cows, the largest Jersey herd in Vermont at that time. It was also the first dairy farm in the area to deliver milk in Fair Haven.

In 1926, Dr. Edward J. Quinn and Charles E. Brough acquired the property and developed it into a resort complex, using the original farmhouse and the large barn, which they named the Annex. It also included the nine-hole Bomoseen Country Club, Tucker's riding stable and a variety of entertainment on Neshobe Beach. By 1930, Pine Cliff Lodge could accommodate fifty guests, including eight in the recently converted barn. It was to be Lake Bomoseen's last new resort. Guests could play a round of golf on the course that began and ended at Pine Cliff Lodge. If golf wasn't their sport, they could go horseback riding, swim at Neshobe Beach or dance in the evening at the Danceland Pavilion on Neshobe Beach. A spacious dining room with hardwood floors was built on the north side of the main lodge, and its large kitchen could accommodate big groups. In the 1950s, Jerry Romania ran Pine Cliff Lodge. Although its restaurant was not on the lake, it was very popular and well-known for its good food. It hosted many wedding receptions and other social events.

This page: Advertisements for Pine Cliff Lodge (June 11, 1966) and Trak II (June 30, 1978). *Courtesy of the* Rutland Herald.

Pine Cliff Lodge changed hands again in 1972, when three men of Italian heritage turned it into an Italian restaurant called La Lago. They created a smaller dining room in the main house and converted the former large dining room addition into a bar and lounge with a dance floor and stage for bands. The new restaurant featured nightly entertainment, and the musicians were often put up for the night in the now-antiquated Annex. But its success was apparently short-lived, as by 1973, La Lago had closed, and its last owners had stripped it of many of the furnishings and equipment. Ownership reverted to the bank, and the buildings stood empty for several years.

In 1975, the bank approached Red and Valerie Poremski, owners of the Trak-In, about purchasing the property. They did, and the couple named it Trak II. Their son worked on getting the new business up and running. The floors were carpeted, except for the dance floor. The walls were covered with old barn board half-way up, with 1970s-style flocked wallpaper covering the rest of the surface. The Poremskis kept the circular bar installed by the previous owners. Trak II was not primarily a restaurant, although light meals or snacks such as pizza and sandwiches were available. Vermont law required bars to serve some food. It was popular for its happy hours and live music. People came to have a drink and socialize with friends, listen to the bands and dance. One popular band was Sea Bird, which was from Massachusetts. Trak II hosted wedding receptions, for which staff was brought in from Trak-In.

At the time the Poremski family opened Trak II, the Vermont drinking age was eighteen, which would lead one to assume the place might be a popular gathering spot for local college students. That wasn't the case, however. The college students were not generally there in the summers when Trak II was open for business. It closed in the winter, as there was no heat. While Trak II was "the place to go" and had a large following, the Poremskis weren't sure how successful it was financially. In 1980, they assessed its finances and discovered that their other businesses—the motel and Trak-In—were carrying Trak II. With additional staff required—bouncers and policeman for parking—plus regular wait staff and kitchen help, entertainment and the expense of running the large pizza ovens, the family decided that keeping Trak II open just wasn't feasible. It closed in the early 1980s. A few years later, the former restaurant and resort was converted into apartments that are still in use today. Perhaps if Trak II had been heated and open year-round, it might have survived.

After the financial assessment that led to closing Trak II, the Poremskis made other changes to their existing businesses. The Trak-In, built in 1973, specialized in steaks and a long salad bar, modeled after the one at the Sirloin Saloon in Rutland. It was the height of popularity for salad bars. The Trak-In was very successful, especially with summer lake residents and visitors to the area. For several years in the 1970s, meals were served in both the old Trakenseen dining room and at the newer Trak-In. This overlapping of meal service ended because of changing times. According to Valerie Poremski, "the younger people were more mobile with their cars, and didn't want to eat all their meals at the same place. The older guests just liked staying there and rocking all day on the front porch." With the closure of Trak II, the family decided to sell any holdings east of Route 30, including the Trak-In. A retired policeman and his wife bought it, with the dream of owning a restaurant on a lake. But they underestimated the amount of work it takes to run such a place, and they kept it only two seasons. The business reverted back to the Poremskis, who held the mortgage, and it has been in the family ever since.

During the early 1980s, the Poremskis had paid off a mortgage on the Trakenseen and remodeled the building. The top story of the 1912, three-story addition was taken off to create a motel with twelve efficiency-type units. Guests staying in any of the accommodations can opt to take their meals at the Trak-In. The restaurant remains one of only three places to eat on the shores of Lake Bomoseen today, and it is run by Roz Poremski Rogers and her husband, Charles. The friendly, efficient service, delicious home-cooked food, extensive menu with many entrees and specials, fresh salad bar, homemade breads and desserts continue to draw a loyal following. Newspaper coupons and daily early-bird specials also draw return customers. The lawn area across Route 30 from the Trak-In hosts summer wedding receptions, and the restaurant is a meeting place for groups and organizations.

A little farther up Lake Bomoseen, near the three major hotels located on Route 30, was where perhaps the greatest concentration of eating establishments could be found during the early part of the twentieth century. The hotels, Cedar Grove, Prospect House and the Trakenseen all provided meals for their guests, but a variety of smaller snack bars and eateries sprang up to cater to both hotel guests and day visitors looking for a light meal or snack. Eddie's on Route 30 was one of these, owned by Eddie Duclos and his wife, Helen. They lived in a small brown house just south of the business.

Hired help stayed out back in a small bunkhouse with no running water. Eddie's was located across from the Catholic Chapel. A 1954 advertisement claimed Eddie's was in its thirty-fifth season, selling homemade Italian pizza, franks, fountain drinks and legal beverages. In addition to fast food—or short order, as it was called then—Eddie's also sold and developed film and offered "sick room supplies." The small brown building that once housed Eddie's remains on Route 30 and is currently in a state of disrepair; it is the last of the former small eating establishments still standing.

Not far from Eddie's, across the road and just north of the Catholic Chapel, on the access road to the Bomoseen Golf Course and the Prospect House, was another small place called the Gatehouse. It advertised steaks, chops, grilled franks, hamburgers and sandwiches, and unlike some other smaller eateries, it had a liquor license. It had a prime location to attract golfers coming off the course for a drink and a bite to eat. The shell of this building existed until 2008, when it was torn down to clear the way for a house being built on the property.

Frank's Place, owned by Frank Duclos, was another small eatery located across from the Tom Thumb miniature golf course. Customers sat at counter stools to enjoy their short order meals of pizza, hot dogs and hamburgers.

One of the Prospect House cottages was turned into a small restaurant called the Sugar Shack. Guests could relax with a drink in a casual atmosphere. The Prospect House management opened it to compete with two other hotels nearby. It later was put on rollers and moved down the hill, where it was added on to the Bomoseen Country Club clubhouse, making it the first restaurant at the golf course. In the beginning, there was only a bar, but a kitchen was added to provide meals and beverages for hungry golfers coming off the links. It has undergone various transformations over the years with different owners. After being vacant for several years, the restaurant reopened during the summer of 2010 as the Prospect House Pub.

A little farther north on Route 30 was Calvi's Grill, opposite the Trakenseen Hotel. It was located where the parking lot for the Trak-In is today. Calvi's claimed to be "still riding the wave of popularity" in the local weekly paper, *Bits o' Bomoseen*, on July 1, 1937. Calvi's had the distinction of long hours; they served breakfast and stayed open until 2:00 a.m. for night owls. Besides the usual fast food, Calvi's had a liquor license and served draft beer, ale and champagne. Like Eddie's, it sold first-aid supplies. Another unusual feature of Calvi's was a lending library for summer visitors' reading pleasure. In the

LUNCHES **ALL LEGAL BEVERAGES**

THE GATEHOUSE

Route 30 — Lake Bomoseen, Vt.

— Your Favorite Stopping Place After Playing Golf —

Wendell Powers, Prop.

This page: An advertisement for the Gatehouse in the July 1957 *Resorter* and a postcard of Frank's Place, dated August 8, 1960. *Courtesy of Castleton State College and the author.*

1950s, Calvi's had doubled its seating capacity, and customers could dance and enjoy cocktails in the knotty pine dining room. It was known not only for its food, but for its friendly, informal atmosphere.

During the 1960s, the Cedar Grove Hotel opened its own alternative dining spot called the Lakeside Cocktail Lounge and Grill. None of the other hotels offered a place where people could get a good meal, cocktails and entertainment in a casual setting. In the 1970s, this night spot became the Somewhere II, an offshoot of the Somewhere Restaurant in Fair Haven. Owner Fred Smith wasn't interested in the old hotel and tore it down.

Across from Cedar Grove Hotel and just north of the Tom Thumb miniature golf course was a restaurant called Ringquist's. In 1978, Gordon and Joanne Ringquist tore down the original home of the Quinlan family, who had run the Cedar Grove Hotel, to make room for a parking lot and renovated the 1937 house that would contain the restaurant. During the twenty years they were in business, all seven of their children helped in various capacities with running the restaurant. During this time, many of the cottages around the lake were locally owned, so the Ringquists depended on summer residents or weekly renters for much of their clientele. Ringquist's soon developed a reputation for good food. It was open year-round, six days a week, and like clockwork on Sundays, "the same people went to the same chairs every week," according to Joanne Ringquist. Early-bird specials, as popular with senior citizens thirty years ago as they are today, drew loyal crowds. During the last few years Ringquist's was open, the owners instituted the policy that "you were never too late for the early bird special."

Ringquist's served a breakfast buffet and also lunch and dinner. Over the years, it catered many weddings and Christmas parties. The employees of Gilmore Lumber and other local businesses came frequently for lunch and often brought clients. Joanne and Gordon both cooked, and one of their sons made breads and desserts. Both had had experience preparing food; Joanne had worked at Royal's Hearthside in Rutland for ten years. Her background there influenced her to include fresh fish on the Ringquist's menu. Ringquist's remained a popular local spot for two decades. Many people enjoyed outdoor dining in the summer on the deck that was added on the north side. However, when the Ringquist children all grew up and left home for other jobs, the senior Ringquists decided to close the restaurant. It was converted back into a family home, and today, one of the sons lives there.

Before closing the restaurant in 1998, the Ringquists started making cinnamon-and-sugar cake doughnuts that they delivered while still warm to local venues, such as Coon's Store, Patty's Patch and businesses in Fair Haven and Poultney. The couple had to get up very early to make the fresh doughnuts and get them delivered for early morning customers at the various locations. Joanne tells a funny story about herself: One Sunday morning, she arrived a little early at one of her customers' stores in Poultney. While waiting

The former Ringquist's restaurant, as it appears today. *Courtesy of the author.*

for the store to open at 8:00 a.m., she began reading the newspaper. But the early hours got to her, and she fell asleep in the car. She was awakened by two young boys' voices.

"Do you think she's dead?" one asked his companion.

"Nah," said the other boy. "She's probably just drunk!"

She made sure that, after making the delivery, she honked her horn at the two boys as she drove away! Often she would be back home by 7:30 a.m. after the first deliveries, and she would start another batch of doughnuts to deliver to other customers. At Patty's Patch, just over the New York state line, her doughnuts were so popular that customers would be waiting for her.

One of the most enduring establishments on Route 30 along Lake Bomoseen was Uncle Charlie's, now known as the Lakehouse Pub & Grille. In 1931, twenty-five-year-old Charles Cillo borrowed money from his parents to open a restaurant on the east shore of Lake Bomoseen between Crystal Beach to the north and the hotels to the south. His nephew helped him construct the restaurant building, which opened on July 4, 1933, as Uncle Charlie's. At one point, Uncle Charlie's had the word "tavern" in its name, but the state of Vermont made them drop it. The four-story building had rooms for the waitresses on the top floor.

Uncle Charlie's Restaurant, 1973. *Courtesy of Chip Ogg.*

The restaurant kitchen and Cillo family living quarters were on the third floor. The second floor contained the dining room. The bait and boat shop was on the first floor. The bait shop was open year-round to cater to ice fishermen as well as regular anglers.

At first, Charles ran the restaurant, bait and boat shop business by himself, but when he married in 1934, his wife, Nickley, helped him. Their children—Mary, Josephine, Paul and Elizabeth—all lived in the family quarters on the third floor, and as each became old enough, they were put to work in the family business. Eventually, running the business took more and more of Charles's time, so Nickley took over the cooking, and she specialized in Italian dishes and fresh lake fish. Charles's easygoing personality, combined with his hard work, made all of his ventures successful, and he was soon known to everyone as Uncle Charlie. The bait and tackle shop thrived as well as the restaurant. Charlie was renowned as an expert fisherman, and he had the reputation of never bringing back a fisherman empty-handed. A 1937 article in *Bits o' Bomoseen* stated that Charlie had adapted a special type of lure—a brown minnow with a red spot on it to attract bass—and it was so successful that fishermen were clamoring for them.

By 1940, Uncle Charlie's had added pizza to the menu, and it was an immediate hit. Charlie's niece, Patsy Ryan Berlickij, recalled that her uncle went to Glens Falls, New York, and brought back dough from a successful restaurant there to start out his own venture with pizza. His pizza became so popular that even visitors from New York City would order pizza to take home with them when they left.

The Cillos prided themselves on fresh ingredients, and to this end, they tried several ventures. They planted a vegetable garden to supply the restaurant and even tried raising their own chickens. Charlie's son Paul recalled one time during the spring thaw when the chicken coops floated away and had to be retrieved by rowboat. When fried clams were added to the menu, Charlie made sure they were fresh through weekly deliveries from Boston.

One improvement Charlie made to the physical structure of the restaurant was the addition of a glassed-in porch overlooking the lake. This remains an attraction today, as patrons can enjoy scenic lake views while dining, even during cool weather when the present-day outdoor deck is not feasible.

By the 1950s, Charlie was getting older, and Nickley had passed away, so he depended more on his son Paul and daughter Elizabeth to keep things going. Elizabeth did the cooking, and Paul waited tables and ran the boat and bait business. The family continued to offer quality food, specializing in fresh fish, Italian dishes and fried clams. During that time period, Uncle Charlie's offered a deal for fishermen: for the paltry sum of twenty-eight cents, one could get a hamburger, a Coke and a dozen worms. Today, that doesn't even buy the worms!

In the 1960s, Charlie added a fiberglass boat to the older wooden rowboats he had always rented out to fishermen. He always referred to it as a "plastic boat," according to Patsy Ryan Berlickij. By the early 1970s, the Cillo family knew the end of an era was at hand. They tried to ease out by shortening the season, opening the restaurant only from Memorial Day through Labor Day, and the bait shop from Memorial Day until Columbus Day. Finally, in 1972, after forty-two years in business, the Cillos sold their business to Charles Ogg of New Jersey. Uncle Charlie was sixty-eight years old by then. He talked about raising trout to sell to other restaurants, but he only lived a short while longer, so his idea never came to fruition.

Charles Ogg, better known to his family and friends as "Chick," and his wife, Maris, closed on the restaurant in December 1972. With three generations of Charles Oggs in the family—Charles Sr., Chick and Chip—the restaurant's existing name was serendipitous. Chick and Maris had always wanted to own a restaurant, and they already had Vermont connections. Chick's father Charles lived in Brandon, Vermont, and Chick was an avid skier who enjoyed Vermont's slopes. The Oggs had no previous experience running a restaurant, but according to their son, Chip, they were "serious foodies" who enjoyed cooking, and they had a strong desire to succeed.

In January 1973, the family—Chick, Maris and their three children who were young adults—Chip, nineteen, Sandy, twenty-two, and Lindy, twenty-five—moved into the restaurant's living quarters. The fourth floor had four bedrooms and bathroom. At that time, the restaurant was on the street level, and the second floor contained the kitchen and an apartment. Chip Ogg surmised that, at one time, the rooms may have been rented out, as they had numbers on the doors and contained room service bells. The bottom floor at lake level held the bait shop and a boat livery.

The Oggs had their work cut out for them. To begin with, like many old restaurant buildings that have gone through several owners and transformations, Uncle Charlie's needed to be brought up to code with new wiring. The Oggs also made extensive renovations to the kitchen, brought the place into compliance with board of health regulations and changed the restroom entrance. The family all worked hard to have the place ready for opening on Memorial Day weekend. That first year, Maris did all the cooking. She prepared gourmet selections such as Coquilles St. Jacques with

Charlie Cillo on a tractor; he's helping the Oggs move in. *Courtesy of Chip Ogg.*

duchesse potatoes, as well as steaks, chicken and fish dishes, lamb and prime rib. Salad bars were coming en vogue, so the Oggs offered fresh salad and vegetables, soup and homemade bread. They aimed to make their clientele feel welcome and added personal touches, such as a free appetizer of bread and a cheese spread with drinks. They continued to have pizza on the menu, which was a popular item.

Chip Ogg was put in charge of the waterfront. To many young people, that would seem like a dream job. However, it was hard work, and he put in long days, opening the bait shop and boat rental at 7:00 a.m., pumping gas all day and closing the restaurant at midnight. The earlier, wooden rowboats were replaced with new fiberglass fishing boats, some with seven-and-a-half horsepower motors, canoes and Sunfish sailboats. The fishing was good, but the restaurant no longer served fresh local fish. In addition to his waterfront duties, Chip helped in the kitchen and did almost anything else around the restaurant that needed doing. During summer heat waves, the kitchen became uncomfortably hot, so sometimes, during a lull, he'd take a break and go waterskiing. After Labor Day, the Oggs closed the business for the season, and that first winter, Chip got a job at Killington Ski Area. There he learned a lot about the restaurant business, and he brought his new

Advertisement for Uncle Charlie's Restaurant, designed by Chip Ogg. *Courtesy of Castleton State College.*

knowledge and experience back to his parents' place the following summer. He went to Castleton State College and majored in business. Chip, along with his sister, Lindy, created the advertisements for Uncle Charlie's.

By the late 1970s, Chip, his sister Lindy and her husband, Sonny Barton, took over the cooking and running of the restaurant with their

Sandy Ogg and friend playing guitar at Uncle Charlie's Restaurant. *Courtesy of Chip Ogg.*

mother Maris's help. Sonny was a musician in a band called Adam, and he also had restaurant experience working at the Back Behind Saloon in Killington. Lindy and Sonny moved into the apartment on the premises. Family members, including Chip's sister Sandy, and friends often provided entertainment at Uncle Charlie's on Saturday nights, playing piano, banjo and guitar. Local groups also performed, such as a singer called the Ozark Whippoorwill and Mark Crowfoot, a local folk singer.

The restaurant featured daily specials, such as pot roast on Tuesdays. In 1975, one could get liver and onions, chopped steak with gravy or chicken dinners for $4.95. Chip recalled getting a workout by running up and down stairs to the walk-in cooler, which was on the street level, one floor above the kitchen. He would remain in the restaurant business until 1995, when he changed careers and became a professional woodworker, handcrafting fine furniture for Charles Shackleton in Bridgewater, Vermont.

In 1979, Chick Ogg sublet the waterfront to Scott Edington, who set up a grill by the dock, a forerunner to the lakeside deck dining available there today. Edington became the sole distributor of the Olympic Class Laser

Fleet, one of only two distributors in the state at the time. These small sailboats were reputed to be among the fastest, and according to an article in the July 12, 1979 *Promoter*, "[they] have been known to pick up enough wind to tow a water skier." Edington's lakeside lunches, served from 11:00 a.m. until 3:00 p.m., were very popular. The lakeside bar was open from 11:00 a.m. until 5:30 p.m. Boaters could gas up, have lunch and pick up bait, tackle or anything else they needed for a day on the water—all in one stop. Today, the Lakehouse Pub & Grille continues to provide the pleasure of dockside dining and entertainment to its patrons, but it no longer has provisions for gas, bait or marine supplies.

Before Scott Edington was involved, a group of young professionals began coming to Uncle Charlie's on a regular basis to go sailing after work, and they often stayed into the wee hours. They began calling themselves "Uncle Charlie's Yacht Club." The fun-loving group called their informal sailing competition "the Fruit Cup." However, as time went on, they became more affluent and acquired larger and more expensive boats, so they eventually relocated to Lake Champlain.

A regular customer at Uncle Charlie's in the mid-1970s was Joe Menoff, the supervisor of lifeguards at Crystal Beach. A powerful swimmer, he'd swim all the way from the beach to the restaurant to have lunch. Joe also operated the weed harvester during that time period, when the battle to keep Lake Bomoseen weed free was already in full swing.

In 1980, the Oggs sold the restaurant to John Mulligan, a former customer who loved Uncle Charlie's and was eager to try his hand at owning it. John Mulligan was a former Vermont state legislator and owner of the Bomoseen Inn in Hydeville. Mulligan renamed it Cap'n John's, thus beginning the restaurant's next incarnation. During renovation, he arrived on a Sunday morning in July 1982 to do some bookkeeping, and he discovered the place was on fire. It took several hours for firefighters to bring the blaze under control. Fortunately, he was able to continue with his plans for the restaurant. Cap'n John's made several improvements, including adding baseboard heat, which enabled the restaurant to remain open year-round. Mulligan himself often sat in a captain's chair with a ship's wheel in front of it. The menu included lobster and crab legs, and the salad bar was set out creatively in a wooden boat. The waitresses wore spiffy blue and yellow uniforms. Parking was—and still is—a problem along that section of Route 30, with rock ledge on one side and a drop off to the lake on the other. Mulligan solved the problem by offering valet parking service. Eric Griffin was one of the car jockeys who took guests' cars down the road to be parked at Crystal Beach and then jogged back up to the restaurant to take care of the next customer. The lower level was unused during Cap'n John's tenure, and boat rentals and bait were no longer available there.

For several years, John Mulligan struggled with a waste problem. He built a large cement holding tank, which had to be pumped periodically. Then he tried pumping it to the other side of Route 30 and up the hill, but neighbors, fearful of possible well contamination, complained. Eventually, the problem was solved when the town sewer line was extended up Route 30.

After John Mulligan passed away, his daughter, Kathy, got Steve and Pam Miller, a young couple, to take over running the restaurant in the late 1980s. The name was changed, once more, to the Dockside. The Millers' management might be considered rather unorthodox. Steve was very busy seeing to his landscape business, which left the running of the restaurant to Pam. She was at home with two young children and trying to juggle child-rearing with managing a business. She would sometimes have to leave to do shopping or other errands, so instead of closing, she left a can on the bar so customers who might show up in her absence could serve themselves and pay using "the honor system." During the winter, the Millers heated the lower level so the Dockside could cater to ice fishermen and snowmobilers. The Millers kept the Dockside going for about five years. Then it reverted to Kathy Mulligan, who decided to sell it "as is."

Kathy Mulligan approached Red and Valerie Poremski, who purchased it in May, 1995, with the idea of converting the building into three apartments. However, they soon discovered they would only be allowed to create two apartments. They decided to restore the restaurant and lease it. By then they had only a few months to comply with existing building codes because they were new owners. Dave Rogers, Red and Valerie's grandson, took on the renovation and running of the restaurant. The restaurant was renamed the Lakehouse Pub & Grille, using the original name of the Trakenseen Hotel. At one point, while the family was bouncing around possible names, Red suggested the Oar House, as he still had a lot of old oars that could be used for decoration. Dave's mother, Roz Rogers, vetoed that idea! Dave improved the dock area to provide lakeside seating, and he also landscaped the grounds. Previous owners had partitioned off part of the bar area, so Dave remodeled it and constructed a new, longer bar from salvaged doors his family had saved from the old Trakenseen Hotel, which was a very fitting use for them. Dave and a high school friend, Greg King, developed a menu and served Vermont beers at the bar. Both men had experience in the restaurant and hospitality business through working at Pico Peak, and Dave had been brought up helping at his family's restaurant, the Trak-In.

The first year the Lake House was open year-round, but they encountered several problems. It was costly to heat, and it was difficult to find room for bands within the confines of the restaurant. Dave and Greg ran the Lake House for nine years. During some of that time, Dave Rogers also served as a state representative in Montpelier.

The Lakehouse Pub & Grille was acquired from Dave Rogers in May 2005 by brothers-in-law Fred Field and Brad Burns. They brought their years of culinary experience to this latest version of the lakeside fixture that started more than half a century before as Uncle Charlie's. The Fields had experience at the Trailside Lodge at Killington prior to purchasing the Lakehouse Pub & Grille. It is a family business, as Deana Field Burns works beside her husband in the kitchen. Courtney Howe Field, Fred's former wife,

Exterior of Lakehouse Pub & Grille, with lighthouse and sail decor. *Courtesy of the author.*

was a server at the restaurant for many years. Her grandmother had lived and worked there back when it was Uncle Charlie's. Today, Brad and Deana Burns run the business.

Since opening in 2005, the bar and two dining rooms have been redecorated, and a band shell was added for summer entertainment. The current owners have maintained the tradition of outdoor dining, the only commercial establishment on the lake that offers it at the present time. The menu offers a blend of American and Pacific Rim dinner entrees, as well as hamburgers and other sandwiches. The bar features many beers on tap and an expanded wine list. One important change is that the restaurant is now open year-round, and the Burnses have used some creative marketing strategies to keep people coming in the normally slow winter season. One winter, they set up a bar on the ice to cater to ice fishing enthusiasts. They also offer specials and a Sunday brunch that attract local clientele and visitors alike.

Local watercolor artist Peter Huntoon has included the Lakehouse Pub & Grille among his subjects for painting. He relates the following amusing story:

> *An older gentleman came in for dinner with a friend and sat at a table near the water. He noticed an attractive server going up the stairs and gestured grandly with his arms that she looked just like an old flame. With the gesture, water glass, napkin and silverware went flying into the lake. The gentleman called to the server and asked for her help. In his enthusiasm, he had knocked his dentures along with his napkin into the water, and could someone help retrieve them for him? The next day, the server donned bikini and mask and rescued the "flying bridge" from Lake Bomoseen. It is not often a man goes to dinner and loses his teeth! The dentures and diner were soon reunited, and the server was properly rewarded for her efforts.*

As you continue north on Route 30, if you make a right onto North Road, just past Pencil Mill Road, you'll find Stable Road on the left. The old farmhouse on the right dates from the mid-nineteenth century. This property was a working farm for many years that raised crops, cows, horses and chickens; but during the 1930s and 1940s, it was run as a guesthouse called Crystal Ledge House. Minnie Murphy served down-home country meals for up to thirty guests at a time and used fresh food from the farm.

Crystal Ledge House, which was later the site of the Stables in the 1960s. *Courtesy of the author.*

"Mrs. Murphy was famous for her cornmeal muffins and huge breakfasts," according to Ed Kaicher, current owner of the property. Crystal Ledge House was open from May until October. Besides the main dining room, there was a rustic cocktail lounge in a detached building from the main house, so any noise wouldn't disturb other guests. The outdoor shuffleboard court can still be seen today, although the markings have long since worn away. Guests were offered an hour of free horseback riding daily, and they could fish in Sucker Brook, which was stocked with trout.

During the 1960s, John and Eileen Brough purchased the old house—the former Crystal Ledge House—and turned the barn into a restaurant called the Stables. They renovated the house and built an addition called the Annex, where the family lived during the summer months while they rented the main house out to guests. The Broughs added a kitchen to the converted barn restaurant and capitalized on the rustic atmosphere. Tables were built into the former horse stalls, and farm implements were used as decorations, with things such as pitchforks turned into coat hooks and mirrors made from old horse collars. The center ceiling light was created from an old wagon wheel. A lounge called the Pony Stall was added to serve guests in off-season months.

Reasonably priced, family-style dinners were served during the summer, with fresh vegetables grown by George Thayer, Eileen's father, or purchased from Brown's Roadside Market in Castleton. The restaurant was truly a family-run business; John's sister, Veronica, made the pies and pastries and helped in the kitchen. All four Brough children—Suzanne, Madeline, John and Tom—also helped out. A typical meal might be half a chicken for $2.50. Steak and pizza were very popular at night. Lunch was available; horseback riders from the nearby Pond Hill Ranch would often stop after finishing a ride. An addition accommodated large groups, such as the local Lions Club,

An advertisement for the Stables in the *Rutland Herald. Courtesy of Castleton State College.*

which met weekly at the restaurant, and it also held its annual Christmas party there. The restaurant hosted wedding receptions, too, and at one, a donkey was ridden into the restaurant. In spite of no live entertainment—only a jukebox—the Stables was very popular. On weekends, it was mobbed with people coming from as far away as Rutland. It was also a place for counselors from the youth camps on Lake Hortonia to enjoy a night out between groups of campers. The atmosphere in both the guesthouse and the restaurant was very casual and informal. The Stables was never locked, and guests were treated like family who were welcome to come across to the restaurant in the morning to make their own coffee. The Broughs used clever newspaper ads to call attention to their establishment. John Brough Jr. recalls the heyday of his family's restaurant business fondly. Eventually, it became too much for the family to keep up with, and it was sold in June 1969, shortly before John Brough Sr.'s unexpected death in August.

As one looks at this continuous parade of restaurants that existed along Route 30, many of them with changing owners, names and appearances, it seems likely that this route along the lake will remain a prime location for eating places. Some of the former dining establishments are completely gone; some have been extensively remodeled and serve as private homes; and just a few exist as restaurants today. A new restaurant opened on Route 30 just north of Castleton Corners in July 2010. It is called Sunrise Family Restaurant and is owned by Peter Burhans. The primary focus this first season will be breakfast and lunch, featuring comfort foods and family fare. They plan to be open for dinner three nights, Thursday through Saturday, with items such as chicken and biscuits, prime rib and turkey dinners.

Chapter 8

THE ROLE OF RECREATION ON THE LAKE IN CASTLETON'S ECONOMY

Fishing

Over the years, the beauty of Lake Bomoseen has been a steady attraction for area residents and seasonal visitors, providing many varied opportunities for local entrepreneurs. For the most part, fishing on Lake Bomoseen has gone hand in hand with boating, with the exception of netting fish at the mouth of tributaries entering the lake. During the late nineteenth century, there were several boat liveries catering to fishermen, notably Mark Bixby's, Theron Goodwin, Ponds and Coffee's Picnic House, which catered to sportsmen and had fourteen boats available. In addition, many of the resorts or hotels also had boats to rent, including Walker's Lake House, Mr. Dunn at the Cedar Grove annex before the hotel was built in 1898 and the Prospect House. Boats could also be rented on Taghkannuc, later officially named Neshosbe Island. Boats were also available for hire at the Russell House and Bull's Fishin' Inn, which became the Edgewater Inn and still exists today.

The typical boat used for fishing during this era was a heavy, curved bottom, wooden rowboat. Fishermen generally used fourteen-foot bamboo poles, since modern casting reels were not yet in use. Some fishermen just used a hand line wrapped around a stick that they jigged up and down to attract the fish. The line itself was not the thin, strong, nylon line of today; it was a black cord or a braided line of macramé cord. At this time, fishermen used only live bait such as worms or minnows. The rowboats could be maneuvered into the weed beds that provided habitat for minnows and smelt, which were the favorite foods for larger fish such as northern pike, large and small mouth bass, yellow perch and sunfish. Some of the larger species like pike and bass preferred shallower areas on the lake's north and south ends.

The popularity of renting rowboats to go fishing ebbed and waned with the times. During the Great Depression, with money scarce for recreation, boat rentals declined sharply. As the economic climate improved, the May 10, 1937 issue of *Bits o' Bomoseen* reported boating was returning to popularity. This continued until World War II, when once again conditions dictated less recreational travel, causing another lull in boat rentals. Once the war was over, the early 1950s saw boating popularity soar to its greatest height. With renewed prosperity after the war, people discovered that owning a boat with an outboard motor was not just a luxury reserved for the wealthy, nor did boating enthusiasts even need to own property on the water. A boat and trailer cost about the same as a low-priced car at the time, making boating affordable for middle-income families.

The Vermont Fish and Game Department has stocked various game fish over the years. In the early part of the twentieth century, Labrador whitefish, walleye and rainbow trout were plentiful, but these have become nearly nonexistent in the lake today because the state no longer replenishes them. Today, brown trout are still stocked, and bass, perch, northern pike and bluegills are caught by anglers on the lake.

From the early 1900s until his death in 1944, William D. "Bill" Bull ran a boat livery at Bull's Landing, located between the Cedar Grove and Trakenseen Hotels on the east shore of Lake Bomoseen. He, with his wife, Anna, and son Howard, operated the Edgewater Inn and lived there year-round. Bill Bull was known locally as a colorful personality. He fed bass from his dock and often entertained visitors by holding a minnow by the tail for his "pet" bass to take out of his hand. His favorite was a one-eyed, old bass he named Old John. Each year, Bill would net Old John and weigh him. In 1941, Old John weighed in at seven pounds, three ounces. Besides renting boats and acting as a fishing guide, Bill Bull worked for Alexander Woollcott, the literary critic and playwright, who spent summers on Neshobe Island with his group of New York cronies, the Algonquin Round Table. He ferried Woollcott's illustrious guests back and forth to the island and was on first-name terms with celebrities such as Harpo Marx, Helen Hayes, Irving Berlin, Vivien Leigh and Laurence Olivier. Bill Bull also took the Neshobe guests on fishing trips. When Alexander Woollcott died in 1943, Bill Bull was one of the first in the area to be notified. He always said he was glad he'd heard Woollcott's last broadcast that evening. Bill passed away the year after Mr. Woollcott. His son, Bill, continued the tradition of providing speedboat rides to hotel guests, and "became quite a Don Juan with the local waitresses with moonlight rides in his speedboat to the center of the lake."

After World War II, fishing equipment began to improve with advances in technology, such as the use of synthetic materials and casting reels that could throw the line farther out in the water. Artificial lures gradually became more popular, especially after a Castleton teenager invented "the Spoon," in 1824. The story goes that Julio Buel accidentally dropped a spoon in the water while eating his lunch out on the lake. He observed a very large fish strike at the spoon as it slowly spiraled to the bottom. He quickly capitalized on this lucky discovery by affixing hooks to spoons, and he had great success in catching bass, trout and northern pike. In 1844, he relocated to Whitehall, New York, and improved upon his invention. He then applied for and received several patents and launched a successful fishing lure manufacturing business in Whitehall.

Fishing has changed on Lake Bomoseen. While occasionally one can spot a solitary fisherman in an aluminum or wooden rowboat or an old "Woodie" power boat, most of the watercraft on the lake today are made of fiberglass. The horsepower has increased exponentially, affording bass fishermen speeds unheard of in past eras. "They [bass boats] developed into fishing machines. Bass fishing has become a national sport, and the bass boat has a look of its own. With engines up to 200 HP, these boats can really move, an important part of fishing tournaments."

The heaviest amount of fishing on the lake occurs during June, July and August as summer residents, tourists and local people hit the water, but the fishing can be good well into October. Once the lake freezes over firmly, usually in January, fishing enjoys a comeback as hardy souls brave the cold, hoping to pull a big one through the ice. This chilly winter sport draws not only area residents, but fishermen from other communities and out of state, all trying to catch a good-sized brown trout, bass or northern pike. Over an extended hard freeze, the frozen surface supports a small settlement, with a variety of colorful homemade shanties offering their occupants shelter from

Ice fishing shanties on Lake Bomoseen. *Courtesy of the author.*

the wind. The ice is also dotted here and there with snowmobiles or pickup trucks whose owners are willing to take a chance on the ice. Woe to the ice fisherman who leaves up his shanty a bit too long—more than one has gone to the bottom of the lake!

Early twentieth-century ice fishing consisted of a handheld line, tip ups and a hand-operated spud to cut through the ice. Today, electric augers do the drilling and a line of tip ups is erected next to the shanty, until an electronic fish finder indicates a school of fish has moved. Some fishermen prefer to use small minnows with their tip ups or tiny lures baited with minnows. Once the hole is drilled, the fisherman hopes he made a large-enough opening to bring out a big one. Age and experience do not always guarantee the most success, as some near-record-size northern pike have been caught by teenagers, who fought for as long as an hour to get their catch out. For many years, the Lake Bomoseen Fishing Derby has attracted fishermen of every description. It is interesting to note the size and variety of fish posted on the derby board each year.

Steamboats

Lake Bomoseen's first steamboat appeared around 1834. It was built by F.W. Whitlock of Poultney and operated from 1834 to 1837. The thirty-five-foot paddle-wheeler had a deck made of black ash and could carry seventy-five passengers. Mr. Whitlock used it for pleasure cruises for two years. He sold it to A.W. Hyde, who continued to use it for pleasure for another year. Then he converted it to transport livestock and to tow barges. People were mistrustful of this new contraption, since it was the first of its kind on the lake, and it did not catch on. In addition, the original Whitlock engine was too small for the vessel. What had seemed like a promising investment proved to be a financial failure. It eventually rotted at its dock.

The pre-Civil War period steamboats disappeared from the lake, but other types of watercraft took its place. In the early 1860s, there was a ferry that went from Coffee's Picnic House on the east shore to West Castleton. Beer's Atlas of 1869 shows a horse-powered ferry with paddle wheels that were powered by four horses on a treadmill. This same sort of boat was used to pull the slate barges to the railroad line near Indian Point and on to Hydeville.

The steamboat *Naomi*, built in Worcester, Massachusetts, was launched in 1877 and was named after the owner's daughter. This small, powerful boat normally would carry up to sixty passengers, but for the July 4, 1881 naming of Neshobe Island celebration, it made numerous trips back and forth from Hydeville to Mason's Point, towing a barge loaded with passengers. That same season, the *Naomi* made regular trips to the resorts, but the following year in 1882, it was not launched because of rumors the boat was unsafe. One Sunday afternoon in 1883, under the ownership of Mike Halloran, the steamer had the misfortune to run up on Black Rock, near Rabbit Island. The captain was able to get the *Naomi* off the rock once passengers disembarked. After that, *Naomi* made regular runs from the dock at Hydeville, with stops at Neshobe Island and Coffee's Picnic House. It operated until at least 1889.

The two most well-known steamers that once plied Lake Bomoseen were the *Arthur B. Cook* and the *A.B. Cook*. Many photos, particularly of the *Arthur B. Cook*, still exist. The *A.B. Cook* was sixty feet long and double-decked, and its steam engine burned pea coal. It operated from 1892 to 1903, transporting passengers from the Hydeville dock to Coffee's Picnic House. The roundtrip fare was twenty-five cents during the week and fifteen cents on Sunday. It

The steamboat *Arthur B. Cook*, with band playing on upper deck, in a postcard postmarked August 30, 1906. *Courtesy of the author.*

left the dock at 1:00 p.m. and returned the passengers at 5:00 p.m. It burned on May 3, 1903, after finishing its years hauling slate for the Lake Bomoseen Slate Company.

The steamer *Arthur B. Cook* was launched on January 9, 1904. It was framed in Albany, New York, and planked in Hydeville. The Dewey and Bliss Carriage Shop of East Poultney had the contract to finish the steamer. This company had expanded from making wagons and carriages to building boats. The new steamer was five feet longer than its predecessor, the *A.B. Cook*, and it had two decks. Owner C.E. Cook named his new vessel after his son, and his daughter christened it with a bottle of brandy that was smashed over the bow. The *Arthur B. Cook* operated for the next twelve years. Upon C.E. Cook's death in 1916, the steamer was sold to Alfred Dagg for $1,750. Unfortunately, it met the same fate as the *A.B. Cook*, burning near Cook's ice house. C.E. Cook also owned another steamer, *Elva*, which was used for transporting passengers and baggage to the hotels. It was eventually converted from steam power to a gasoline engine, and it, too, ended its days transporting slate for the Lake Bomoseen Slate Company.

Other early boats on Lake Bomoseen are worth mentioning. A smaller, nineteen-foot steamer, the *Thistle*, accommodated about ten passengers and was used as a pleasure yacht. Another early boat was called the *Harry M.*

Bates. Its steam engine ran on naptha gas, which was used to create steam instead of the usual pea coal. It could carry up to seventy-five people. On July 24, 1891, the *Poultney Journal* reported the *Harry M. Bates* was busy all day Sunday, and "in the different trips up and down the lake carried over 300 passengers. This steamer now makes two regular trips daily from Hydeville, connecting with both the morning and evening trains." In August 1890, it was reported that the *Harry M. Bates* was prevented from picking up passengers in Hydeville due to low water in the creek, but people were transported to and from the hotels by horse-drawn wagon. The *Harry M. Bates* is believed to have sunk just off the Prospect House's dock. Another naptha gas-powered, three-cylinder engine boat was the thirty-six-foot *Cygnus*. It was used for passengers and to haul slate, but its engine was found to be unreliable. Owner C.E. Cook sold *Cygnus* to hotel owner W.C. Mound in 1908 for $400.

A unique boat that sailed on two area lakes, Lake Bomoseen and Lake St. Catherine, was a canopied sightseeing craft known as the *Water Wagon*. In 1912, Walter Brown and Ace Hayes built two of these boats. The pilot's wheel was mounted toward the stern of the boat, with the Ford Model T engine within easy reach in front of the pilot. Both water wagon boats were launched on Lake Bomoseen. One was sold, and the other was used on Lake

The *Water Wagon*, going past Cedar Mountain. *Courtesy of Rick Wilson.*

Bomoseen for years. It eventually was moved to Lake St. Catherine, where it remained active for well over forty years, into the 1950s. This remaining *Water Wagon* became the centerpiece for the recreation center known as Idylwild. Walter Brown built the pavilion at Idylwild Park in 1915, and based the *Water Wagon* there, operating the boat for twenty-six years. After some years of disuse, Cliff Ellis restored the *Water Wagon* in 1948 and operated it for another six years. Once again, it fell into disuse, lying neglected on shore with its canopy riddled with holes. The July 8, 1966 *Resorter* ran a story about the old *Water Wagon* and suggested someone restore it as a memorial to the past. Evidently, no one has taken up this suggestion.

Regattas

Beginning in the early twentieth century, regattas have been held on Lake Bomoseen from time to time. In 1905, the Lake Bomoseen Yacht Club held its first regatta, which became an annual event until 1915. That year, seventy-three boats in thirteen different categories participated. In 1908, Daniel E. O'Brien entered his boat, the Pauline, in the regatta. The following year, *Pauline* took first place for the best-decorated boat.

The *Pauline*, as entered in the 1908 regatta. *Courtesy of Judy Crowley.*

The day of the fourth annual regatta, in August 1909, was an ideal day with a crowd of about three thousand spectators. Businesses closed in Fair Haven so that merchants and employees could attend. The crowd gathered at the Cedar Grove Hotel to watch the three-mile race of single and two-cylinder engine motorboats. The *Fair Haven Era* reported the race didn't start until 3:00, by which time many of the large crowd had begun to lose interest. The winner, *Rescue*, owned by J.H. La France, took twenty-nine minutes to complete the course.

By the fifth regatta in 1910, in addition to seventy-five boats participating, a contest with prizes for the best-decorated boat was part of the parade. There were also swimming contests and canoe races. However, by 1914, the decorated boat parade was dropped by decision of the Lake Bomoseen Yacht Club, due to lack of interest and participation.

The tenth-annual regatta and water carnival of 1915 was the last one for many years until the Lake Bomoseen Association (LBA), which was formed in 1954 by a group of property owners, revived it in 1957. LBA member Getty Page was the organizer for the event, which included a boat parade with prizes for the best-decorated inboard and outboard boats and a water-skiing carnival. The boats in the parade ended up in front of the Prospect House to be judged and awarded prizes.

Decorated "chicken boat" from the 1913 regatta. *Courtesy of Polly Dolber.*

In 1958, there were several different boat races, and the rival Lake Bomoseen Boat Club sponsored a regatta. This group of boaters was made up of people who were not lake property owners. Former marina owner Lloyd Bronson recalls that each boat in this regatta flew a pennant emblazoned with an Indian head.

After another hiatus of some years, the July 4 boat parade was revived in 1997 by the Lake Bomoseen Association. In addition to numerous private pleasure boats decorated with patriotic themes, there was a large pontoon boat that provided music over a loudspeaker. The following year, the *Fair Haven Promoter* advertised that the Bourbon and Blues Band would perform live at the start of the parade at the Woodard Marine dock. In the evening, D.J. Frank Antun provided music for dancing after a picnic supper at Crystal Beach. It also became customary for lakefront property owners to affix lighted flares to their docks for "Light up the Lake" on July 4. Castleton's Concert on the Green live concert series holds a Fourth of July concert at Crystal Beach, followed by fireworks sponsored by the Lake Bomoseen Association. This event has become very popular, with hundreds of people watching the fireworks from their boats just off Crystal Beach or along the shore. One year, just as the fireworks were to begin, a thunderstorm rolled over the mountains from the west, causing boats to scatter in every direction, a potentially dangerous situation, but fortunately no collisions or mishaps were reported.

During the 1950s through the early1980s, the Lightning Fleet no. 227 was a very active sailboat club that held races on the lake and sometimes hosted other clubs. The nineteen-foot Lightning series sailboat is designed for racing and has been manufactured since the 1930s, first with wooden hulls and then lighter-weight fiberglass. At the height of its popularity, Lake Bomoseen's Lightning fleet numbered in the thirties, but by the mid-1980s, the number had fallen off. On August 1, 1982, the *Rutland Herald* reported on a two-day race on Lake Bomoseen involving sailboats from Vermont and New Hampshire. Each year, sailboat skippers and their three-person crews from these two states met to compete at a major lake in one state or the other. "Hazy skies produced a diabolical mixture of stiff breezes and dead calm to challenge the 23 sailors who plotted a seven-leg course of about five miles across the roiling waters." The summer 1984 issue of *Vermont Life* magazine proclaimed, "Sailing has become an enormously popular sport on Lake Bomoseen, and regattas are held throughout the summer. It is not unusual these days to see twice as many sailboats as motorboats."

During the 1970s, catamarans called Hobie Cats became en vogue on Lake Bomoseen. They were easily identified by their large, colorful sails. The "Cats" could achieve twice the nautical speed of the Lightning sailboats, and in a good wind, they seemed to fly across the lake. Hobie Cats remained popular for about ten years, with regattas held on Lake Bomoseen, but these were eventually supplanted with a new sport, sailboarding, during the 1980s. A spinoff from waterskiing and surfing, sailboarding involves standing on surfboard-like hull topped with a mast and sail. Obviously this sport involves more stamina and a supreme sense of balance, particularly during the races that Lake Bomoseen enthusiasts organized. Sailing never really goes out of popularity and can always be seen on the lake, but today, with the increasing number of smaller sailboats manufactured and their relatively easy transport, it is enjoying a resurgence of interest.

Marinas and Other Boating Businesses

Until the middle decade of the twentieth century, most boats on the lake were small, family runabouts with low horsepower outboard engines. A few inboards could be found, and wooden or aluminum rowboats remained popular for fishing and recreation. As time went on, however, people began to want more power, and more services were needed by boat owners. By the mid-1950s and early 1960s, this increased interest in boating led to the creation of a number of boat-related businesses. In 1951, Lloyd Bronson Sr. purchased the old slate factory at the southeast end of Lake Bomoseen, where he established the first sales and boat rental shop on the lake. At first, Bronson's Boat Shop built rowboats and repaired Chris Craft boats. Bronson was a skilled craftsman, and he later built small hydroplanes in the late 1950s. He also sold and repaired Johnson motors and stockpiled hard-to-find parts for older engines, such as Scott Atwater and McCullough. Lloyd Bronson Jr. recalls that if anyone was looking for a piece of mahogany with which to repair a boat, his dad would likely have one somewhere in the shop. When Lloyd Jr. and his brother returned from the military, they decided to reorganize the shop's parts department, putting everything in alphabetical order. Lloyd Sr. had a fit because he couldn't find anything!

During the 1950s and 1960s, Lloyd Sr. designed and built about two hundred boats, many of which remained on Lake Bomoseen waters.

The New QUIET
MERCURY OUTBOARDS
Authorized Sales & Service
GLASTRON, MIRROCRAFT
DURATECH BOATS

- Shore Station Boat Hoists
- Full Line Marine Accessories
- Expert Boat & Motor Service & Repair
- Texaco Marine & White Gas.

THE BEST BOATING BEGINS AT

WOODARD MARINE

• on Lake Bomoseen
State Park Rd at Hydeville — Tel. 265-3690

SWING INTO FAMILY FUN

Mercury Outboards
Authorized Sales and Service
— BOATS —
Glastron, Glassmaster, Duranautic, O'Day
Sail Boats and Old Town Canoes
Shore Station Hoists — Snowco Trailers
Excellent Line of Marine Accessories
Boat and Motor Repair
Texaco Marine and White Gas

WOODARD MARINE

State Park Rd. on
Hydeville, Vt. Lake Bomoseen Tel. 265-3690

Bronson's Boat Shop

Custom Boat Building
Repairing
Hydeville, Vt.
Gas and Oil Rentals
On
Bomoseen Canal
Ph. Fair Haven 317-M4

Advertisements for Bronson's Boat Shop and Woodard Marine in the *Resorter* on August 27, 1965, and August 25, 1967. *Courtesy of Castleton State College.*

During that era, boats were generally built of wood or aluminum with small outboard engines. A few had Chris Craft inboards, and fiberglass boats were beginning to gain popularity. Water sports like tubing and waterskiing were not yet as popular as today, so most people didn't need high-powered engines. Even with this in mind, Lloyd Bronson Jr. believes the total number of boats on the lake during his father's heyday was greater than it is today.

Bronson boats were renowned for their excellent craftsmanship. They were easily recognizable on the lake, as most were painted a light marine "Bronson Blue." In 1962, Lloyd Sr. moved the business across the channel into an old house renovated for the purpose, with the workshop on the ground floor. Lloyd Bronson Sr. was in business until the 1970s. After his wife became ill, he sold the business and it became Kip's Wharf. Under the new name and ownership, it continued boat sales, rentals and service. Today, Kip's Wharf is part of Woodard Marine.

For almost ten years, Bronson's Boat Shop was the only marina on the lake. In 1960, Woodard Marine opened for business on the channel just south of the Route 4 highway bridge. The Bronson and Woodard marinas were friendly competitors; Woodard sent people needing service on Johnson motors to Bronson, and in turn, he sent Mercury owners to Woodard. Both of these marinas included boat sales and rentals, repairs, dock rentals and gasoline sales.

In addition to Bronson's and Woodard's marinas, several other boat-related businesses existed around Lake Bomoseen. By the 1960s, more and more boat owners who did not own waterfront property needed a spot to dock their boats. Bronson's could accommodate fifty boats, and Uncle Charlie's Restaurant near Crystal Beach also rented dock space. Some enterprising lakefront owners who had unused space rented out docks; Theresa Larkin on Creek Road was one. By 1963, Woodard Marine had space for forty boats.

Duda Water Sports has been in business for forty-two years on Creek Road just north of Hydeville. Owner Walter Duda rents all kinds of boats from fishing boats to pontoon boats. Walter says he has seen many changes during his years on the lake, but he still considers it the most beautiful lake in the region.

In 2005, Rob Steele purchased Tom's Bait and Tackle Shop from Eva Evanoika, whose late husband, Tom, started the business in 1973. As a high school and college student, Rob helped Tom at the bait shop. It is open all year long, except during the month of November, and it sells everything for fishing from live bait to tackle. Ice-fishing season is their busiest time of year.

Today, custom-made boats are very costly, so the majority of boat owners purchase their boats from national manufacturers through boat dealerships, but this was not always the case on Lake Bomoseen. Lloyd Bronson Sr. had built numerous custom boats during his years in business, and in 1963, the Woodards built four racing boats with thirty-five horsepower engines. A year later, Raymond Woodard began building a drag boat that he nicknamed *That Damn Thing* because every time he needed more money for it, his wife, Rowena—known as Chris—would say, "You need money for that damn thing again?"

The Woodard family was no stranger to boat building. Around 1910, Frank Woodard, Ray Woodard's uncle, quit working for the Taylor Boat Company in Quebec and set up his own shop, the Woodard Boat Works, with his four sons. Raymond Woodard came to work for the Woodard–McCrea Boat Company in the 1920s. They built racing boats such as the Hacker Pelican 151 in Hatley, Quebec. As he gained experience in the 1930s and 1940s, Ray Woodard built a few boats on his own. After World War II, he moved to Chester, Vermont. There he founded Woodard Marine and worked full time at boat building. His boats were well-built, with white oak frames, plywood hulls and mahogany decks. By 1954, the hulls were covered with fiberglass. At the height of production, his boat company built about eighteen runabouts, twelve to sixteen feet long, per year. Some still exist today and are highly prized. They were displayed at Woodard Marine's fortieth anniversary event.

Raymond Woodard's sons, Robert and Alan, grew up in their father's boat business and learning the skills; later, both men built twenty-six AE Haekercraft and twelve AE Penn Yan replicas. When fiberglass boats became the norm, Ray Woodard decided to switch from boat building to sales. In 1961, he and his wife, Chris founded Woodard Marine on the south end of the lake in Hydeville. At first, the family lived in Fair Haven, but in 1962, they built a home next to the business. In its first decade, Woodard Marine dealt exclusively with Mercury motors, but in recent years they have expanded to sell a variety of different makes and models.

By 1968, Ray Woodard was ready to relinquish some of the running of the business to his sons, but he did not officially retire until 1976. Ray and Chris bought a cottage on Indian Point where they resided summers until

A boat built by Ray Woodard on display at the fortieth anniversary of Woodard Marine. *Courtesy of the author.*

they passed away. They wintered in Florida for a number of years. In the summer, they could be seen zipping across the outlet in their boat to help out at the marina.

Today, Woodard Marine has continued to expand. Besides its main facility north of the Route 4 bridge on Route 4A, it acquired the Lake Bomoseen Marina once owned by Vito and Mary Guarino; that site is now the boat rental center for Woodard Marine. Sadly, Alan Woodard passed away on July 10, 2001, but Bob Woodard, his wife, Barbara, and their daughter Lauren Woodard-Splatt and son-in-law Eric Splatt work full time at the marina. Bob and Barbara's older daughter Danielle Budlong and son Greg help out when they're available. Today, watercraft that would be unfamiliar a generation or two ago are very popular. Large, stable-platform pontoon boats have become increasingly common. Known more for stability than speed, they are popular with families for relaxation, entertaining and even fishing. Personal watercraft such as jet skis is particularly popular among younger people. Easily transported by trailer, they can be purchased or rented at Woodard Marine. Woodard Marine continues to provide a wide variety of services. Because of the destructive power of the lake ice as it breaks up in the spring, dock owners have to remove their lifts and docks each fall. Woodard Marine provides a boat lift service that tows the lifts to the marina for the winter. It also shrink-wraps and stores boats for the winter in its large storage facility on the premises. The store at the marina sells all kinds of boating supplies and accessories, as well as water sports-related equipment. Woodard Marine sponsors social events for customers each summer. It is the only boat-sales business on the lake today, and it also is the only place where boats can be refueled. Woodard Marine celebrated its fiftieth anniversary in 2010. It is a five-star dealership and has been voted one of America's top one hundred dealerships.

There is another boat repair business, also on Creek Road, not far from Route 4A, called Engine Joe's Marine Repair, which is owned by Joe and Liz Kent. Joe has lived in the area all of his life. He began his career in engine repair at age seventeen, working for other marinas for twenty-one years before establishing his own business in 2005. Besides routine engine repair jobs, Joe builds custom outboard motors for stock outboard racing and restores classic outboard engines.

Chapter 9

CASTLETON'S STRUGGLE TO SLOW THE AGING OF LAKE BOMOSEEN

Lake Bomoseen is contained within two towns, Castleton and Hubbardton, and the economies and tax bases for both towns are supported by lake property owners, as well as by residents in other areas of these two towns. The lake also draws summer residents, fishermen, boaters and visitors to the area, supporting local businesses. It might be considered the most important natural resource in the area. Therefore, it is in the towns' interests that property values around the lake remain stable. To this end, the quality of the lake itself must remain high.

Thousands of years ago, Lake Bomoseen was carved out by glaciers and filled in with clear water as it melted. Over the millennia, plant life decomposed, and organic and mineral material gradually began to affect the water clarity. This normal aging process that takes place in a body of water is known as eutronication. Over many thousands of years, a lake can gradually become a wetland, then a swamp and finally dry land.

Today, Lake Bomoseen is almost seventy feet deep at its deepest point, between Neshobe Island and the Bomoseen State Park on the west shore. But much of the lake is no deeper than twenty feet, allowing native aquatic plants to thrive and providing prime habitat for sport fish such as bass. Native water plants, which boaters and fishermen may consider a nuisance, are generally beneficial to a lake. The wetland area north of the Grady Float Bridge is a good example. The plants act as a "nutrient trap" that filters and absorbs nutrients and cleans the water that is flowing south from northern tributaries.

By the early 1970s, native aquatic plants were being crowded by the proliferation of an invasive non-native plant, Eurasian milfoil. Runoff from the shoreline encouraged the rapid growth of weeds in the shallower and warmer areas of the lake, interfering with swimming and boating. People became concerned about the quality of the lake, which was shown by well over thirty articles in the *Rutland Herald* from 1974 to 1984 on a wide range of related topics such as water pollution, water levels, weed harvesting and chemical weed control.

Even before this time, in 1963, James Leamy—a third-generation Lake Bomoseen resident, Town of Castleton health officer and executive director of the Lake Bomoseen Association—was hired to do a sanitary survey of the lake to identify pollution sources. The survey found several large hotels were discharging fifteen to twenty gallons of wastewater daily into the lake, and at least thirty private cottages were contributing to the pollution. The State of Vermont and the Town of Castleton attempted to alleviate the pollution by running a sewer line along the east shore to the hotels and requiring permits for private homeowners to install septic systems. In 1972,

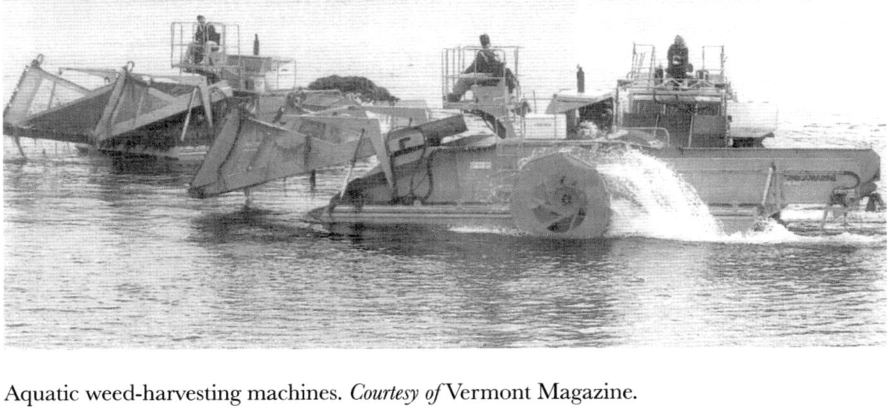

Aquatic weed-harvesting machines. *Courtesy of* Vermont Magazine.

a waste treatment plant was built south of Castleton Corners to handle the sewage. Ironically, the hotels were not destined to remain in operation for too much longer, even with the new sewer lines. One by one, the Prospect House, Cedar Grove and the Trakenseen closed. The state monitored water quality for some years afterward, so that by 1981, the lake had an acceptable water quality.

While pollution was coming under control, the weed problem remained a difficult one to solve. In 1974, the Vermont Water Resource Department recommended weed harvesting as the most effective means of control. In addition, fifty acres of the lake were treated with chemicals. The State of Vermont did not agree with chemical treatment, arguing that it only created more problems when the dead weeds sank to the bottom and fertilized the next year's crop, along with any possible negative impact on fish or other wildlife. So, in 1975, Castleton and Lake Bomoseen property owners paid a Cambridge, Massachusetts, company one hundred dollars per acre to harvest one hundred acres of the weed-infested areas of the lake. The Town of Castleton used an Environmental Protection Agency grant to purchase and maintain three weed harvesters a year or two later. The weed harvester was a sort of floating thresher with a conveyor belt that sent the cut weeds into the stern, much like a lawn mower with a bagger. The weeds were transferred onto dump trucks and sold at a nominal fee to farmers for fertilizer.

The weed harvesting program was met with mixed reviews. It became increasingly more expensive for the town as time went on, especially with reduced state funding and fewer members in the Lake Bomoseen Association, which had footed part of the bill. Boaters liked it. Fishermen felt weeds supported the bass population, and the harvester didn't discriminate between milfoil and native plants. Homeowners worried the cut weeds would merely serve as fertilizer for more weeds as they floated toward shore and sank to the bottom. The last year of weed harvesting was 1995. Since then, weed growth has fluctuated, with some seasons showing heavier growth than others.

Another attempt to control the proliferation of milfoil during the 1990s was the introduction of a weevil, *Euhrychiopsis lecontei*, which prefers milfoil over native plants, into Lake Bomoseen and nearby Glen Lake. According to an article by Tom Mitchell in the June 13, 1993 issue of the *Rutland Herald*, scientists didn't feel the weevil would "appear to pose a risk to fish, wildlife or humans." It burrows into the plant stem, causing it to collapse and sink. It showed some success in several Vermont lakes, including Lake Bomoseen.

Some other area lakes, Lake St. Catherine as an example, are using limited chemical control at the present time. Careful monitoring of discharge into the lake to limit the amount of nutrients available for the weeds seems necessary to help control the problem, but the milfoil continues to thrive. Some lake property owners have taken matters into their own hands. According to Jim Leamy, the weed harvester operator noted that milfoil suddenly would disappear in front of one cottage or another, undoubtedly the result of applying illegal chemicals obtained out of state.

Another controversial topic regarding the management of the lake has been whether to draw down the water level in the fall. The level can be controlled through use of a dam, now owned and managed by the State of Vermont, at the end of the outlet. Some property owners favored the lake level be dropped to minimize ice damage to their docks and shorelines, while others, especially on the north end, objected that their waterfront would look like a mud flat. The battle waged for years, but finally in 1983, the state stepped in and decreed Lake Bomoseen would be maintained at "plus or minus three inches" year round, citing the need for duck nesting grounds on the north end and pointing out that the lower lake levels created a greenhouse effect conducive to weed growth in the spring. The last

The dam at the southern outlet to Lake Bomoseen. *Courtesy of the author.*

major drawdown happened in 1988, when the state inspected the dam and replaced the 1920s-era gates. The retaining walls also were upgraded, and the dam was fenced to discourage its use as a local favorite swimming hole. This happened after two youngsters were swept through the spillway in a powerful undercurrent. Fortunately, they survived without serious injury.

Today, one of the major contributors to the aging of Lake Bomoseen seems to be manmade. Clear cutting along the shoreline for development has created an erosion problem. In 1974, a group of Crystal Beach area residents petitioned the Town of Castleton about the problem of their dock area at the mouth of Sucker Brook being filled in with silt from development projects. While the developer was eventually ordered to stop further work, the "Delta," as the residents call it, continues to spread with winter and spring storms that wash debris and more silt down to the lake.

To sum up the ongoing problems and controversies among local and state governmental agencies, residents and users of the lake, perhaps Virginia Garrison, a supervisor with the Vermont Water Resource Department, said it best back in 1981: "A lot of people seem to want their lakes to be a bathtub. They don't care about what the lake should be…Pattern your use of the water to what the lake should be, and minimize man's impact on the lake."

BIBLIOGRAPHY

Beck, Ronald. "An Interview of Rose Parsons on the Pencil Mill," Senior paper, Castleton State College, May 2, 1970.

Bits O'Bomoseen. "Boating Popularity Increasing," May 10, 1937.

Castleton Historical Society. *Castleton Looking Back.* Castleton, VT: Castleton Historical Society, 1998.

Doran, Joseph. "Slate Quarries in Vermont." Unpublished, 1998. Castleton Historical Society Archives. Castleton, Vermont.

Fair Haven Era. "Bomoseen House and Ransom Store Go Up in Smoke," November 7, 1912.

———. "Castleton Has a Disastrous Fire," August 5, 1915.

———. "Largest Business (Union) Block Totally Destroyed," July 21, 1904.

Fair Haven Promoter. "Bomoseen Boat Parade," July 2, 1998.

———. Checkmate Restaurant advertisement, July 6, 1989.

———. Prunier's Market advertisement, July 27, 1995.

Fowler, Arthur. "Boating and the Boating Industry on Lake Bomoseen, 1870-1970." Senior seminar paper, Castleton State College Archives, 1991.

"A History of Castleton Vermont." *Vermont Historical Gazetteer* 3 (1877).

Hogan, Shannon. "The Steamboats on Lake Bomoseen." Senior seminar paper, Castleton State College, 1990.

Jordan, Holman D. Jr. "Coon's Store: The Coon Family and Other Enterprises." Unpublished. Castleton Historical Society, Castleton, Vermont, 1981.

Lauf, Walt. "Ice Fishin' Straight from the Fish's Mouth." *Castleton Newsletter* 1, no. 34 (February 1999).

Patry, Matthew J. "Brown's Roadside Market: A Family Tradition for 70 Years." Senior seminar paper, Castleton State College, 1987.

Petty, Terrence. "Bomoseen, the Lay of the Lake," *Vermont Life* 38, no. 4 (Summer 1984).

Pistorius, Alan. "The Milfoil Mess," *Vermont Magazine* 5, no. 1 (January–February 1993).

Poultney Journal. "Steamer Harry M. Bates," July 24, 1891.

———. "The Vermont Pie Belt," August 30, 1909.

Read, Iris Hopson. *Lake St. Catherine, A Historical Scrapbook*, 2nd ed. Poultney, VT: Lake St. Catherine Association, 1998.

Resorter. Coon's Store advertisement, August 21, 1954.

———. Crystal Ledge House advertisement, August 21, 1954.

———. Gatehouse advertisement, August 6, 1954.

———. Nesto's Market advertisement, August 21, 1954.

———. Woodard Marine advertisement, August 25, 1967.

Rogers, Frank F. "Vermont Slate Leads the Nation in Quality, Second only in Quantity," *Vermont Life* 10, no. 2 (Winter 1955–1956), 5.

Rutland Herald. "Apple Growers in Two Counties Begin Harvesting Crop Valued at $350,000," September 14, 1939.

———. Birdseye Drive-In Diner advertisement, May 28, 1941.

———. "Bomoseen Yields Weeds to an Underwater Mower," June 14, 1975.

———. Hawaiian Luau at Johnny's advertisement, August 8, 1972.

———. "Lakes' Bacteria Levels 'Good,'" July 9, 1981.

———. "Lightning Fleet Race," August 1, 1982.

———. Patricia's Restaurant advertisement, June 18, 1976.

———. Pine Cliff Restaurant advertisement, June 11, 1966.

———. Pioneer Lodge advertisement, July 16, 1949.

———. The Stables Restaurant advertisement, August 13, 1966.

———. Trak II Restaurant advertisement, June 30, 1978.

———. Uncle Charlie's Restaurant advertisement, July 4, 1974.

Slate History Trail. Montpelier: Vermont Agency of Natural Resources, Vermont Department of Forests, Parks and Recreation, January 1988.

"The 'Spoon' Lure, Born on Lake Bomoseen." *Castleton Newsletter* 1, no. 50 (July 2000).

Steele, Reverend Joseph. *History of Rutland County, Vermont.* White River Junction, VT: White River Paper Co., 1882.

Sutton, Charles, and Catherine Sutton. *Roxies Famous French Fries, the Story, the Fries, the Fifty Years.* Poultney, VT: The History Pages Co., 20008.

Thompson, Zadock. *History of Vermont, Natural, Civil and Statistical.* Burlington, VT: Chauncey Goodrich, 1842.

Towers, Jerome. "A History of Staso Mining." Unpublished. Castleton Historical Society, Castleton, Vermont, February, 1978.

Waite, Frederick C. *The First Medical College in Vermont, Castleton 1818–1862.* Montpelier: Vermont Historical Society, 1949, 123–125.

Westcott, Coulman. "Bomoseen Recollections." *Fair Haven Promoter*, July 20, 1995.

————. "Bomoseen Recollections." *Fair Haven Promoter*, July 27, 1995.

Woodard, Alan. "40 Years Have Past." *Castleton Newsletter* 1, no. 26 (June 1998).

INDEX

D

E

F

G

H